MACMILLAN
INTERMEDI

GW00370618

RUTH RENDELL

A New Lease of Death

Retold by John Escott

MACMILLAN

MACMILLAN READERS

INTERMEDIATE LEVEL

Founding Editor: John Milne

The Macmillan Readers provide a choice of enjoyable reading materials for learners of English. The series is published at six levels – Starter, Beginner, Elementary, Pre-intermediate, Intermediate and Upper.

Level Control
Information, structure and vocabulary are controlled to suit the students' ability at each level.

The number of words at each level:

Starter	about 300 basic words
Beginner	about 600 basic words
Elementary	about 1100 basic words
Pre-intermediate	about 1400 basic words
Intermediate	about 1600 basic words
Upper	about 2200 basic words

Vocabulary
Some difficult words and phrases in this book are important for understanding the story. Some of these words are explained in the story, some are shown in the pictures and others are marked with a number like this: ...³. Phrases are marked with ᴾ. Words with a number are explained in the *Glossary* at the end of the book and phrases are explained on the *Useful Phrases* page.

Answer Keys
Answer Keys for the *Points for Understanding* and *Exercises* sections can be found at www.macmillanenglish.com/readers.

Contents

A Note About The Author   4
A Note About The Story   6

1 'He Was Hanged ...'   8
2 Henry Archery   15
3 'He Wasn't a Murderer'   21
4 The White Mini   26
5 Mrs Josephine Crilling   30
6 Alice Flower   37
7 'The Most Beautiful Dress ...'   42
8 Ten Thousand Pounds   46
9 The Change in the Law   54
10 Faces at a Funeral   61
11 The Surprise Alibi   67
12 'I've Cut Myself!'   71
13 'She's Covered in Blood!'   76
14 The Truth   81

Points for Understanding   85
Glossary   89
Useful Phrases   95
Exercises   96

A Note About The Author

Ruth Rendell is famous for writing psychological thrillers[1] and murder mysteries. She is often called the 'Queen of Crime'. Her novels often focus on the complicated reasons why people commit[2] crimes and how crime affects people. Her novels featuring Chief Inspector Wexford are very popular and many of the stories have been made into television programmes which are shown in countries across the world. They star the British actor George Baker as Wexford.

Ruth Rendell was born Ruth Grasemanne on the 17th February, 1930 in South Woodford, London. Both of her parents were teachers. Her father was British and her mother was Swedish. Sadly, her mother died while Ruth was still young.

The author began her writing career as a journalist, working for newspapers in Essex. During this time, she met and married another journalist, David Rendell, and the couple have a son.

Her first book, *From Doon With Death*, was published in 1964. It introduced Chief Inspector Reginald Wexford and he soon became one of crime fiction's most famous detectives.

Ruth Rendell has also written a number of novels under the pen-name (or pseudonym[3]) of 'Barbara Vine'. Barbara is Ruth Rendell's middle name. Vine was the name of her great-grandmother.

The Barbara Vine novels are generally longer and more detailed than the Ruth Rendell stories. They don't always have a murder in them and they are often set partly in the past.

Ruth Rendell has won several awards and prizes for her work, including the Crime Writers' Association Diamond, Gold and Silver 'Daggers', and the *Sunday Times* Literary Award. She has also won the Mystery Writers of America Edgar Allen Poe Award. In 1996 she was awarded a CBE (Commander of the

British Empire), an honour[4] given by the Queen for services to Britain.

Ruth Rendell is now in her 80s but she still writes every day. She has written more than 60 novels which have sold over 20 million copies. Her books have been translated into more than 25 languages worldwide and many have been made into TV programmes and films.

A Note About The Story

Chief Inspector Reginald Wexford lives and works in the fictional mid-Sussex town of Kingsmarkham, in south-eastern England. When some of the stories were televised, the town of Romsey in Hampshire was chosen for filming because it was very much like the 'Kingsmarkham' of the Ruth Rendell stories. Kingsmarkham is how many people imagine an English market town – pretty and picturesque, with a beautiful church and plenty of wonderful countryside nearby. Wexford is also very much like an English country-town policeman. He is more interested in people and the reasons for their crimes than in forensic evidence[5] or 'clues[6]'.

A *New Lease of Death* is set in the mid-1960s. It was a time before mobile phones, when television pictures were in black and white and The Beatles were the world's most famous pop stars.

In the past in the UK, murderers were often killed for their crimes. However, capital punishment[7] had been suspended in 1965, and was finally stopped completely in 1969. Murderers now faced life in prison instead of death.

In *A New Lease of Death*, Wexford is forced to look again at the first murder case of his career – the murder of an old woman called Rose Primero, in 1950. Her murderer had been caught and hanged, but now someone starts asking questions about the person who was convicted[8]. Was he *really* the killer, or could it have been someone else? The person asking the questions has important reasons of his own for wanting to prove[9] that the convicted killer was innocent.

A note about class

Although she was quite poor when she died, Mrs Primero came from a very rich family, who had lived in a large country house called Forby Hall for hundreds of years. England used to

6

have a strong 'class system' – different levels of society that did not usually mix. Rich, usually educated people were known as 'upper class'. Often, this class of people did not need to work to earn money. They lived in big houses with a lot of land and they employed servants to take care of them.

Professional people who had qualifications[10] from school, college or university, such as policemen, nurses, clergymen and teachers, were described as 'middle class'. Wexford, the Archerys, the Kershaws and Detective Inspector Burden are all middle class.

The Painters, Alice Flower and the Crillings are all 'working class' – they do not have qualifications or training and they depend on the money they earn.

Mrs Primero thought that she was better than the people who worked for her. She did not want her grandchildren to play with Tess because she said she was not 'the right sort of child'. Mrs Primero thought of herself as 'a lady' – someone from a rich, educated family. She looked down on[P] other people who did not have the same kind of family as she did. Henry Archery also looks down on others. For example, he believes that his son may be 'too good' for Tess because her father is a murderer.

In this novel, Ruth Rendell looks at how class affects people and their attitudes. She also shows how a person's class can change and that – underneath their class – people are not always what they seem to be.

A note about the title

The phrase 'a new lease of life' refers to the time when a person who has perhaps been ill or unhappy starts a new period of their life with hope and energy. This is usually because something good has come into it. We might say a new pet or relationship has given someone 'a new lease of life'. The title of this Reader is therefore a 'play' on words. Although the person in the story has been dead a long time, questions bring the case back to life.

1

'He Was Hanged ...'

It was five o'clock in the morning, and Detective Inspector Mike Burden was standing by the window of Chief Inspector Wexford's office. Outside in the corridor[11], Burden could hear Wexford saying good night – or good morning – to Mr Griswold, the Chief Constable. Minutes later, he saw Griswold's car drive away.

Burden turned round when Wexford came into the room. The Chief Inspector was a big, powerful-looking man with a loud voice. He was tired and his heavy grey face looked a little greyer than usual after the long night.

'Griswold's just given me this,' said Wexford, sitting down in a chair. He showed Burden an envelope. 'It's a letter he received from the Reverend Archery.' Then Wexford took a letter from the envelope and unfolded it. 'All Griswold told me was that this Archery is a good friend of his, and the letter is about "that terrible man Painter". I'll have to answer it.'

'Who's Painter?' asked Burden.

'He was a murderer who was hanged fifteen or sixteen years ago,' Wexford replied.

Burden looked over the Chief Inspector's shoulder as he read the letter aloud.

Dear sir, You will remember the case[12] of Herbert Arthur Painter. I understand that you were in charge of[13] it so I decided to come to you before making my enquiries[P].

'What does he mean, "enquiries"?' said Burden.

'I don't know,' said Wexford. 'He's going to phone me this morning. It was the first murder case I ever investigated[14] on my own,' he went on, angrily. 'There's no mystery. Herbert Arthur

Painter killed his ninety-year-old employer by hitting her over the head with an axe[15]. He did it for two hundred pounds.'

'She was killed in her own home, wasn't she?' said Burden. 'One of those big old houses off the Stowerton road?'

'It's called Victor's Piece,' said Wexford.

'I think I know it. It was an old people's home until last year. It's very run-down[16] now – I suppose it will be pulled down.' Burden tried to remember the murdered woman's name, but couldn't. 'What was she called?' he asked.

'Rose Isabel Primero,' said Wexford. 'When she was a child she lived at Forby Hall – her family had owned the place for hundreds of years.'

Burden knew Forby well. 'Perhaps Archery is her relative,' he said.

'I don't think so,' said Wexford. 'The only relatives old Rose Primero had were her three grandchildren. Roger Primero, her grandson, lives at Forby Hall now but he didn't inherit[17] it, he had to buy it.'

'There was a family called Knyaston at Forby Hall,' said Burden. 'But that was many years ago.'

'That's right,' said Wexford. 'Mrs Primero was born a Knyaston. She was nearly forty when she married Dr Ralph Primero. They came to live at Victor's Piece when he retired. They weren't rich. When the doctor died in the 1930s, Mrs Primero was left with only about ten thousand pounds. There was one child, a son, but he died soon after his father.'

'Was Rose Primero really still living alone when she died?' asked Burden. 'Even at such[18] an old age?'

'She had a maid[19],' said Wexford. 'Alice Flower. She's still alive. She was about seventy when Mrs Primero was killed. Alice had been with her for fifty years. She and Painter were both Mrs Primero's servants, but Alice sometimes gave him his orders.'

'Was Alice frightened of Painter?' asked Burden.

'Painter killed his ninety-year-old employer by
hitting her over the head with an axe.'

'She hated him,' said Wexford. 'He was employed by Mrs Primero as a driver and gardener. After the doctor died, Mrs Primero and Alice Flower tried to manage without help. But by 1947 Mrs Primero was in her eighties and Alice was nearly seventy. Also, the old lady never did anything, it was all left to Alice. Mrs Primero wasn't an easy person to work for.'

'Or to like?' said Burden.

'Probably not,' said Wexford. 'When she was too old to go to church, she made Alice go instead. *Made* her. When her son died, he left his wife and kids without much money. Mrs Primero said that she was happy to help them, but only if they came to live with her. But she loved her grandson, Roger, and she had one good friend. I'll tell you about her later.

'There was a garage with a large room over the top of it in the gardens of Victor's Piece,' Wexford went on. 'Mrs Primero put an advertisement in the *Kingsmarkham Chronicle* for a young man to work in the garden and drive the car. He could live in the flat above the garage. Mrs Primero had the room divided into three rooms. A lot of people answered the advertisement, but she chose Painter for the job.'

'Was his wife employed by Mrs Primero, too?' asked Burden.

'No, only Painter. The child – her name was Theresa, I think – was only two years old. Mrs Primero didn't want her in the house with her mother.'

'Not a nice woman,' said Burden. 'What about Mrs Painter?'

'She was very pretty and quite small. She was a bit afraid of her husband.'

'So Mrs Primero and her maid lived alone at Victor's Piece,' said Burden.

'Yes,' said Wexford. 'The garage was about thirty yards from the back door of the big house. Painter only went up to the house to carry in the coal[20] and get his orders.'

'Oh, yes, the coal,' said Burden. 'Wasn't there something important about that?'

11

'Painter was supposed to[21] cut wood and to carry coal up to the house at mid-day and again at six-thirty in the evening. He always complained about it because he didn't like going out to get it on winter evenings. He wanted to bring all the coal for the day at eleven o'clock in the morning, but Mrs Primero wouldn't let him do that. She wanted him to bring some in the morning and some in the evening. Do you want me to go on?'

Burden nodded.

'By September 1950,' said Wexford, 'Painter had been working for Mrs Primero for three years, but he was always asking her for more money. He knew that she kept money in the house.'

'And an old handbag containing *the* two hundred pounds,' said Burden.

'Yes,' said Wexford. 'It happened on the evening of September 24th, a cold wet Sunday. Mrs Primero had sent Alice to church. She left at about quarter past six. Painter brought the coal in at six-thirty – and left with two hundred pounds. Mrs Primero was found at seven o'clock. She was lying on the living-room floor near the fireplace in a great pool of blood. There was blood on the walls and on her chair, and there was an axe in the fireplace. It, too, was covered in blood.'

Suddenly the phone rang and Wexford stopped to pick up the receiver. When he had finished listening, he said, 'Archery's coming at two o'clock.'

'What's it all about, did he say?' asked Burden.

'He'll tell us this afternoon,' said Wexford. 'I've got to go out, but I'll meet you for lunch at the Olive and Dove Hotel.'

———

It was just before one o'clock when Burden arrived at the hotel. Wexford came in five minutes later. They talked over lunch.

'Mrs Primero died without making a will[22],' said Wexford. 'Remember I told you that she'd only got ten thousand pounds?

That was divided between Roger and his two younger sisters. He's a rich man now, but he didn't get his money from his grandmother. He's a businessman.'

'How old is he?' asked Burden.

'He was twenty-two when his grandmother was killed which means he must be about thirty-eight now. The sisters were younger. Angela was ten and Isabel was nine.'

'Roger spoke at the trial[23], I remember,' said Burden.

'Roger visited his grandmother that Sunday,' Wexford said. 'He was working in a solicitor's[24] office in Sewingbury and often had Sunday tea at Victor's Piece. Roger took his little sisters there a few times, and they were all very happy together.'

'Old people usually like kids,' said Burden.

'They had to be "the right sort of children". Angela and Isabel, yes. And she liked young Elizabeth Crilling.'

Burden stared at him. 'Elizabeth Crilling?!'

'Don't you remember? Elizabeth – who was five years old at the time – found Mrs Primero's body,' said Wexford. 'She didn't come to the trial because she was too young.'

'No, I don't remember. I'd only just left school,' said Burden. 'But I don't understand. You said Mrs Primero only liked "the right sort of children"? She thought Elizabeth Crilling was "*the right sort of child*"? Elizabeth who is now always in trouble with the police? Her mother's half crazy and they live in Glebe Road.' Glebe Road was in one of the poorer, rougher[25] parts of the town. 'They have no money. How could Mrs Primero have known *them*?'

'In September 1950 Mr Crilling was still alive and the Crillings lived opposite Victor's Piece,' said Wexford. 'Mrs Crilling was about thirty and not "half crazy" at the time. A woman called Mrs White lived next door to her.'

Burden remembered the two small white houses in the lane. 'But that means Mrs Crilling isn't fifty yet,' he said. 'Well, she looks much older.'

'Mental illness always makes a woman look much older,' said Wexford. 'Mrs Crilling has been in and out of mental hospitals for years.' He looked at his watch. It was 1.45pm.

'How did Mrs Primero and the Crilling woman become friends?' asked Burden. 'I suppose they *were* friends?'

'Oh, yes,' said Wexford. 'Mr Crilling had been an accountant which, in Mrs Primero's opinion, made his wife a "lady". Mrs Crilling often visited Victor's Piece, and she always took Elizabeth with her. The child called Mrs Primero "Granny Rose", like Roger and his sisters.'

'So she "visited" that Sunday night and found Granny Rose dead?' said Burden.

'Mrs Crilling had made a party dress for Elizabeth,' explained Wexford. 'She finished it at about six o'clock. The child put it on, and they went to show it to Mrs Primero. Mrs Crilling waited until Alice had left for church because Alice didn't like her.

'It was about twenty minutes after six,' Wexford went on. 'But Mrs Primero was asleep and Mrs Crilling didn't go in. She just knocked on the living room window. When the old woman didn't wake up, she went away and returned later. Importantly, she noticed that there was *no coal* in the fireplace, so she knew that Painter hadn't been in.'

'So Painter came in and killed the old woman between Mrs Crilling's visits,' said Burden.

'She and the child didn't go back until seven o'clock,' replied Wexford. 'They went in by the back door, called "hello!" or something, and walked on into the living room. Elizabeth went in first.'

'And saw the body!' said Burden. 'Terrible! So what's Archery's connection with all this?'

'We shall soon know,' said Wexford.

2

Henry Archery

Henry Archery was not dressed like a vicar[26]. He wore a light-coloured suit and tie. He was very good-looking with thick fair hair and tanned skin.

'I want you to tell me that Painter may not have been guilty,' began Archery.

Wexford shook his head. 'Painter killed her,' he said.

'Why are you so sure Painter was guilty?' asked Archery.

'Do you have the trial transcript with you?' asked Wexford.

Archery took the papers from an old leather briefcase. For five minutes, Wexford looked at them silently, then he looked at Archery.

'We have to think back to Saturday, September 23rd,' Wexford said. 'The day before the murder. Painter didn't appear with the coal. The two old women waited until nearly eight o'clock. By then the fire was almost out. Alice Flower was angry and went out to get some coal herself.'

'That was when she hurt her leg,' said Archery quickly.

'It wasn't serious, but Mrs Primero blamed Painter,' said Wexford. 'She sent Alice to fetch[27] him the next morning then Alice heard Painter and Mrs Primero arguing in the living room.'

'Painter talked about the argument at his trial,' said Archery. 'He says that at first Mrs Primero threatened[28] to dismiss[29] him, then she agreed that he needed to be paid more money. But she refused to increase his salary – she said that he would only ask for another increase in a few months' time. Instead she agreed to give him a bonus[30].'

'I remember all that,' Wexford said impatiently. 'He said that she told him to go up to her bedroom and get her handbag from the wardrobe. There was about two hundred pounds in the handbag. She said he could have the money and take it away in the handbag.' He coughed. 'I didn't believe him and neither did the jury[31].'

'Why not?' Archery asked quietly.

Wexford sighed. 'Firstly, the stairs at Victor's Piece go up between the living room and the kitchen. Alice Flower was in the kitchen cooking the lunch but never heard Painter go up the stairs. Secondly, Mrs Primero would never have sent the gardener upstairs to look around her bedroom. She would have sent Alice for the handbag.'

'Perhaps she didn't want Alice to know about the bonus,' said Archery.

'Of course she didn't,' said Wexford. 'But she would have found an excuse to send Alice for the bag without telling her about the money. And thirdly, Mrs Primero was very mean with money. Alice had been with her for fifty years without ever getting a bonus. Also, we know that Painter needed money. The night before when he didn't bring the coal, he had been drinking in a pub with a friend from Stowerton. The friend offered to sell Painter his motorbike for just under two hundred pounds. Painter asked his friend to keep the bike for two or three days, until he could get the money. If Painter was given the money before mid-day on Sunday, why didn't he phone or go and see his friend on Sunday afternoon? There's a phone box at the bottom of the lane. We checked with the friend. He didn't leave his house all day and the phone never rang.'

'If Painter went to the wardrobe after he killed Mrs Primero, why was there no blood inside the wardrobe?' asked Archery.

'He probably wore gloves to kill her,' said Wexford. 'Or he could have knocked her unconscious[32] with the axe and taken the money. Then he came downstairs, panicked[33], hit her again and killed her.' He looked at the transcript again.

'Painter said that he went to get the coal at half-past six that Sunday evening. He said that he cut up some wood and cut his finger. And he did cut his finger – deliberately[34].'

'You went to talk to Painter after the crime was discovered?' said Archery.

'Yes. We were at his flat above the garage by quarter to eight,' replied Wexford. 'Painter was out. Mrs Painter said that he came back from the big house some time after half-past six and went out again straightaway. He told her that he was going to Stowerton to see his friend. We'd been there ten minutes when he came in. His story sounded false and there was too much blood around to have come from a cut finger. I arrested[35] him immediately.'

'At the trial,' Archery said, speaking slowly, 'Painter said that he hadn't been to Stowerton. "I waited at the bus stop," he told the jury, "but the bus never came. I saw the police cars turn into the lane and wondered[36] what was happening. My finger was bleeding a lot and I came back to my flat".'

Wexford answered him patiently. 'I was in one of the police cars. We went past the Stowerton bus and turned into the lane. There was nobody at the bus stop.'

'You believe that Painter was hiding some clothes when he said that he was at the bus stop?' said Archery.

'Yes,' replied Wexford. 'When Painter was working, he usually wore a raincoat. Sometimes it was in the garage, sometimes it was hanging behind the back door of Victor's Piece. Painter said that he hadn't worn it that evening but had left it on the back door. Both Alice and Roger Primero remembered seeing it there that afternoon, but Mrs Crilling was certain that it wasn't there at seven o'clock.'

'You finally found the raincoat under a hedge[37] two fields away from the bus stop, didn't you?' said Archery.

'Yes,' replied Wexford. 'The raincoat, a sweater and a pair of gloves, all covered in blood.'

17

'But anyone could have worn the raincoat, and you couldn't identify the sweater.'

'Alice Flower said that it looked like one of Painter's sweaters,' said Wexford.

'What about Painter's wife?' asked Archery.

'A wife cannot be made to give evidence against her husband,' Wexford reminded him. 'She didn't appear at the trial. She and the child went away somewhere. Two years later I heard that she was married again.'

Archery leant forward. 'That child is now twenty-one and a very beautiful young woman,' he said. 'I have a son, my only child, who is also twenty-one. He wants to marry Miss Painter. Or Miss Kershaw, as she is now. They met at Oxford.'

'At the *university?*'

'Yes,' said Archery. He smiled. 'Miss Kershaw is a very intelligent young woman.'

Wexford was amazed. Usually, children who have such a bad start in life continue to have problems. He would have thought Painter's daughter would be lucky if she had become a simple manual[38] worker and avoided too much contact with the police. Instead, she had everything: intelligence, advanced education, beauty, and she was in a relationship with a vicar's son.

'Mr Archery, are you sure that this *is* Herbert Arthur Painter's daughter?' asked Wexford.

'Of course I'm sure,' said Archery. 'She told me. She came to stay with us in June. We liked her immediately, and we could see that she and our son really loved each other. "There's something you need to know," she told us. "My father's name was Painter and he was hanged for killing an old woman." My wife couldn't believe it but Charles said it didn't matter[P]. He said people are what they are, not what their parents did. Then Tess said, "It would matter if he had done it, but he didn't." Then she began to cry.'

'Why does she call herself Kershaw?' asked Wexford.

'It's her stepfather's[39] name,' said Archery. 'The Kershaws have two children of their own, but Mr Kershaw gives Tess as much love and kindness as his own son and daughter. Chief Inspector, Tess knows that her father didn't do it – her mother told her that she knew for certain[P] that he didn't do it.'

Wexford smiled. 'People believe what they want to believe. I'd probably say the same thing if I were her.'

'Tess says that her mother never talks about Painter, never discusses him at all,' said Archery. 'She just says quite calmly, "Your father never killed anybody".'

'You think that Painter gave his wife some sort of proof that he was innocent?' said Wexford. 'How could he? Apart from the few minutes when he came back to the garage to wash his hands – and hide the money – he was never alone with her. And he couldn't have told her then because if he was innocent then he would not have known that Mrs Primero was dead. He could have told her that he'd done it, but he couldn't have told her that he had not done it. Then we came and found the blood in the kitchen where he'd taken off the sweater. When he came back, we were with the two of them until we took him away.'

'She must have seen him in prison,' said Archery.

'Only when a prison officer was with them,' said Wexford.

Silently, Archery took a photograph from his pocket and put it on the desk. The picture showed a boy and girl standing in a garden with their arms round each other. The boy was smiling, and he was obviously Archery's son. The girl stared sadly into the camera with large steady eyes.

'I hope she'll make your son very happy.' Wexford gave the photograph back to Archery.

Both anger and pain were in Archery's eyes. 'I don't know who or what to believe,' he said. 'And until I do, I can't agree with the marriage.'

'And the girl, Painter's daughter?'

'She accepts that others may not believe in her father's innocence,' said Archery. 'And I don't think that she would marry my son while his mother and I feel the way that we do. Every time we looked at our grandchildren, we would be looking for the face of a murderer!'

Wexford said quietly, 'I wish that I could help you, Mr Archery, but the case is closed, finished.'

––––

'What did he want, sir?' asked Burden.

'For me to tell him that Painter was innocent,' said Wexford. 'And that it was OK to go and talk to all the witnesses[40] in the case.'

'And his only reason is Mrs Painter's belief in her husband's innocence?

'Yes. There's no other reason for it. Wouldn't you do the same to protect your children? She's developed this idea to protect her daughter, and now she believes it herself.'

'Has he ever met Painter's wife?' asked Burden.

'Not yet,' replied Wexford. 'But she and her second husband live in Purley and they've invited him for tea.'

'You say that the girl told him in June – that was nearly two months ago. Why has he waited so long?'

'Archery said that he and his wife just wanted to give their son the chance to change his mind. But he didn't. He made his father get the trial transcript and speak to Griswold. Archery promised to investigate as soon as he got two weeks' holiday.'

'So Archery will be back,' said Burden.

3

'He Wasn't a Murderer'

Number 20 Craig Hill was a large red brick house with a colourful, well-kept[41] garden. A boy, who looked about twelve years old, was washing a car outside the house.

Archery got out of his own car. 'Is this Mr Kershaw's house?' he asked.

'Yes,' the boy replied. He looked very much like Tess, but his hair was fairer.

'My name is Archery,' said the vicar.

A tall, thin man came out of the open front door. 'Good afternoon, Mr Archery,' said Kershaw, smiling. 'I've been waiting for you. Come inside and meet my wife.'

Archery tried to guess Kershaw's age as he followed him into a square hall. He was perhaps forty-five, forty-six? Kershaw took him into the living room.

'This is my wife,' Kershaw said. 'Irene, this is Mr Archery.'

Irene Kershaw was dressed very neatly in a knee-length skirt and blouse. Around her neck hung a pearl[42] necklace. She smiled but said nothing. Her face was Tess's face, but older.

'Sit down, Mr Archery,' said Kershaw.

Archery sat in an armchair by the window. He looked quickly around the room, noticing how clean and comfortable it was.

'We were pleased to meet Charles,' said Kershaw. 'I liked him.'

'We all like him,' Irene Kershaw said suddenly. 'But will they have enough money when they get married? Charles doesn't have a job, and ... where will they live?'

Archery was amazed. Was she really worrying about such unimportant things?

'Is tea almost ready, Irene?' Kershaw said.

'Oh, yes,' she said. Then she got up and left the room.

'Mr Archery, I know you haven't come here just to meet us and have tea with us,' said Kershaw. He smiled. 'But I can't tell you anything about Tess's father that wasn't in the newspapers at the time.'

'Perhaps her mother – ?' began Archery.

'She and I want to see Tess get married and be happy,' said Kershaw. 'But I'm not sure that Tess can be happy with a man who thinks she might be a murderer's daughter.'

'It isn't like that!' said Archery, quickly. 'He thinks that Tess is perfect. I'm the person asking the questions. He doesn't even know that I'm here.'

The door opened. A girl came in with cups and plates and put them on the small table. She was about fourteen years old. Her mother followed her with a plate of cakes and a teapot.

'This is my daughter Jill,' said Kershaw.

Jill sat in a chair and Mrs Kershaw began to pour tea into the cups.

'You must have one of these cakes, Mr Archery,' said Mrs Kershaw. 'Jill made them. She and Tess are good cooks. Tess will be a good wife for your son.'

'I'm sure she will,' said Archery. 'Mrs Kershaw, I wanted to speak to you alone.'

Irene Kershaw seemed to grow smaller in her chair. She put down her cup and plate and looked at her hands. Kershaw looked at his daughter.

'Jill, you know all about Tess,' he said. 'Mummy has to talk with Mr Archery.'

'OK,' said Jill.

Her father put his arm round her and took her into the garden.

Archery had to begin, but he was hot and felt awkward. Mrs Kershaw looked at Archery then quickly looked away.

'Tess says that you have something to tell me,' he said, quietly. 'About your first husband.'

Mrs Kershaw put her hand up to the pearls around her neck. 'I never speak about him, Mr Archery,' she said. 'The past is the past.'

'I know it's painful – it must be,' he said. He was quiet for a moment, then went on, 'I've been to Kingsmarkham today and ...'

'I was born near there,' she said. 'It's a funny, sleepy little village. I expected to live and die there, but you can't know what's going to happen in your life, can you?'

'Tell me about Tess's father,' said Archery.

She was silent for several moments, then she looked at him. 'As I said, the past is the past, Mr Archery. I know it's difficult for you to understand, but I really can't speak about it. He wasn't a murderer. Her father was a good kind man who wouldn't have hurt anyone.'

'But how do you know?' he said. 'How *can* you know? Mrs Kershaw, did you see something or hear something?'

The necklace was tight in her hand now. Suddenly it broke and the pearls fell onto the carpet. She gave a little laugh. 'Look what I've done!' she said. She began to pick them up and Archery helped her. 'I'm really looking forward to the wedding Mr Archery. Are you? I –'

Just then a ball hit the window and she hurried across to open it. 'Now stop it, Jill!' she called. 'I don't want a broken window!'

Archery looked at her. She was angry. 'You can't have a quiet discussion when there are children about, can you?' she said.

And suddenly the whole family was in the room again. Jill was looking bored and angry, the boy was asking for his tea, and Kershaw was smiling.

'Jill, you can come and help me in the kitchen,' said Mrs Kershaw. She turned to Archery as she reached the door. 'I'll

The necklace was tight in her hand now. Suddenly it broke and the pearls fell onto the carpet.

say goodbye now, Mr Archery. You've got a long journey and I know you must want to get home … if we don't meet again before the wedding – well, I'll see you in the church.'

The door closed. Archery did not move.

'Do *you* believe her?' he asked Kershaw.

'It's different for me,' said Kershaw. 'I don't care, you see.'

'But I care,' said Archery.

'But who will know about Tess, if you don't tell them?'

'I shall know,' said Archery.

'Why worry?' said Kershaw. 'Tess won't marry your son if you don't want her to.'

'And how will Charles feel about me then?' Archery said angrily. He tried to calm himself. 'Your wife is absolutely *sure* of the father's innocence?'

'She's always been sure,' said Kershaw.

'Then I shall go back to Kingsmarkham,' said Archery.

4

The White Mini

The young man lay on his back on the pedestrian crossing[43] in the middle of the road. Burden got out of the police car and looked round. He saw an ambulance, and he saw the white Mini at the side of the road with its front light smashed. A doctor was standing next to the young man lying on the crossing.

'It's very bad,' the doctor told Burden. 'I think his back's broken and there are internal injuries.'

Burden looked across at the car. He recognized that Mini. A girl was sitting in the front seat, leaning forward with her head in her hands. Her hair was short and black and she had pushed her fingers through it. He could see her long red fingernails.

'Don't worry about her,' the doctor said angrily. 'She's not hurt.'

Burden turned towards the small crowd of people at the side of the road. 'What happened? Did anybody see it?' he asked.

A man with a dog looked down at the young man lying in the road. 'He looked right and left,' he said, 'but there was nothing coming. He started to walk across the road when that white car ...' He shook his head. 'The driver, that girl, she was going like a crazy thing ... sixty miles an hour, perhaps more. The car hit him, threw him up in the air, and ... that's all.'

A woman touched Burden's arm. 'He wants a vicar,' she said, pointing at the young man. 'He keeps asking for Father Chiverton. I think he knows that he's dying.'

'Chiverton is the vicar here,' said the doctor. 'But he's away on holiday.'

Burden walked over to a police constable. 'Gates,' he said, 'go into Stowerton and get a vicar.'

'We've tried Stowerton, sir,' said Constable Gates. 'No luck. But there's a vicar with the Chief Inspector now. I could contact the station and – '

'Do that,' said Burden, and he walked across to the Mini.

———

The girl was crying, but not because of the accident. It was because of the photograph that she had seen two hours earlier, in the estate agent's window. It was nearly three years since she'd last had the nightmare. Now those terrible dreams were going to begin again and she didn't have to be asleep to have them.

It was a photograph of a house. *The* house. Not as it was now, dirty and run-down, but how it had been long ago. After seeing it, she had got into the Mini and driven to Flagford to drink away the memories.

But they would not go away.

The detective inspector was coming towards the car, his eyes full of anger.

———

Wexford looked at Archery. 'Do you really think that you're going to find out anything new after all this time?' he asked.

Archery thought about the question. Did he think these things could not happen to anyone he knew? Did he really know what a murderer's child would be like, and that she could not be like Tess?

They were in his office. Wexford was sitting at his desk, with Archery opposite him.

'I just want to go and see Alice Flower,' said Archery. 'And I'd like to talk to Roger Primero and the other grandchildren.'

Wexford sighed. 'All right,' he said. 'Alice Flower is in an old people's home in Stowerton.'

He got up from his chair and walked across to a wall map.

'Stowerton's there,' he said, pointing with his pen. 'Victor's Piece is about here, between Stowerton and Kingsmarkham.'

'Where can I find Mrs Crilling?' asked Archery.

'In Glebe Road, but I can't remember the number.' Wexford stared at Archery. 'You're wasting your time, of course.'

'Chief Inspector, I don't want to accuse[44] anyone else of murder, I just want to prove that Painter was innocent,' replied Archery.

'But you cannot find innocence without finding guilt somewhere else,' said Wexford.

Sergeant Martin appeared at the door. 'A white Mini has knocked down a man in the High Street, sir,' he told Wexford. 'He's dying and they want a vicar. Gates remembered that Mr Archery was here.'

Archery looked at the sergeant. 'I'll come now,' he said.

'A white Mini? I think I'll come with you,' said Wexford.

———

The crowd had gone, but there were still several policemen with the dying man. Archery looked at the Mini, but looked away quickly when he saw the blood on the broken light.

He turned towards the young man and heard himself say, 'It will be all right'.

The young man tried to speak, but blood was coming from his mouth and Archery couldn't understand what he was saying. Archery started to say a prayer[45].

'You can stop now, he's dead,' said the doctor after a few minutes.

Archery stared at the dead man for another moment, then turned away.

He went to ask Wexford for the name of a hotel, a place to stay that night. Wexford was talking to the girl in the Mini.

'This is bad,' he heard Wexford say. 'This is very bad, Miss Crilling.'

'So that's the girl who found Mrs Primero's body?' said Archery to Wexford as they walked over the bridge a few moments later.

28

'That's Elizabeth Crilling, yes,' said Wexford. 'One of Kingsmarkham's wild young people. A boyfriend gave her the Mini for her twenty-first birthday.'

Archery was silent. Tess Kershaw and Elizabeth Crilling were the same age and they had played together in the fields behind Victor's Piece when they were children. At that time, the Painters had been miserably poor but the Crillings had money and lived in a nice house.

'Mrs Primero was *too* nice to her,' said Wexford. 'She gave her sweets and toys. After the murder, Mrs Crilling was always taking Elizabeth to psychiatrists. She went to several different schools and she was always in trouble, always in court for doing something bad.'

'But it was Tess whose father was a murderer,', thought Archery. 'You could have expected *her* to grow up like that, but instead she had gone to a good school and then on to university.'

'I really want to talk to Mrs Crilling,' said Archery.

'Come to the court in the morning,' said Wexford. 'She'll probably be there.'

5

Mrs Josephine Crilling

Two people sat in the public seats of Kingsmarkham courtroom – Archery and Mrs Josephine Crilling. Archery looked at her – Mrs Crilling had a sharp, thin face and long grey hair. She kept looking nervously at her daughter, Elizabeth, in the court below.

'Elizabeth Crilling, I have no choice,' began the magistrate[46]. 'You drove your car when you had been drinking alcohol and now a man is dead. I must send you for trial at the higher court in the town of Lewes.'

Mrs Crilling jumped up. 'You can't put her in prison!' she shouted. 'You're not going to put my baby in prison!'

Without thinking, Archery moved next to her. At the same time, a court policeman went quickly across to the woman. 'Please come outside,' the policeman said.

Josephine Crilling pushed him away. 'Get away from me!' she screamed. Then she turned to Archery and said, 'You've got a kind face. Are you my friend?'

Archery was embarrassed. 'You can ask for bail[47],' he said.

'*Bail!*' shouted Mrs Crilling. 'This man is my friend! He says that I can have bail!'

The magistrate gave Archery a cold stare. Then he turned to Elizabeth Crilling. 'Do you want to ask for bail?' he asked, and the girl nodded.

A policewoman went over to Josephine Crilling. 'Come with me,' she said, calmly. 'Let me take you to get a cup of tea.'

She took Mrs Crilling out of the courtroom and, minutes later, Elizabeth was given bail and allowed to leave the court.

Wexford and Burden had also been in the courtroom, and they left together.

'You're not going to put my baby in prison!'

'Remember when we had to take Mrs Crilling to the mental hospital at Stowerton?' said Wexford. 'Archery may start to wish he hadn't been such a "friend" to her when she begins to shout and scream at him.'

They met Archery outside.

'Good morning, sir,' Wexford said to Archery. 'Terrible thing that accident last night. I was just telling Detective Inspector Burden about a similar accident twenty years ago. A young man was killed out at Forby, hit by a lorry. He was saying something about a girl and a child before he died. He asked for a vicar, too. But he died before the vicar got there. I've never forgotten it. The young man's name was John Grace. He –'

At that moment, the policewoman came up to Wexford. 'Mrs Crilling gave me this letter for a Mr Archery.'

'Take my advice and throw it away,' Wexford told him, but Archery had already opened the envelope.

> *24a Glebe Road, Kingsmarkham*
> *Dear sir,*
> *They tell me that you are a man of God. God has sent you to me and my baby. I will be at home this afternoon, waiting to thank you.*
> *Your friend,*
> *Josephine Crilling*

––––––

Archery's bedroom at the Olive and Dove Hotel was large and very comfortable. He sat down on the edge of his bed and telephoned his wife.

'Henry!' she cried. 'I've been trying to call you! I've had a letter from Charles. Tess phoned her parents yesterday evening and now she's told Charles that she can't marry him! She says that it wouldn't be right. And Charles is threatening to leave Oxford and go overseas.'

'Oh, no!' said Archery.

'There's a lot more in the letter,' his wife said. 'I've got it here.' She began to read: *'I've studied the case myself and there are lots of questions to answer. There was an inheritance, but it was not spoken about at the trial. Three people received a lot of money after Mrs Primero died and one of them was at Victor's Piece the day that she was killed. I think that Father could get the police to re-open the case. Why doesn't he try harder?'*

'Now listen, dear,' said Archery. 'Write back to Charles and tell him that Tess is being very sensible. Say that I'm having some very interesting talks with the police and I'll do my best.'

After he had put down the phone, Archery went down to the hotel dining room. After a minute or two, the door from the bar opened and a man and a woman came in. The man was small and dark and the woman with him was tall. Both were well-dressed[48].

Archery looked away and began eating his lunch.

———

Later, Archery found number 24 Glebe Road. He pushed open the gate and saw that there were two doors to the house, not one. It was two tiny flats. He knocked at the door of 24a and waited. At first nothing happened. Was Josephine Crilling asleep? Then the door opened and Elizabeth Crilling appeared. It was obvious that she was going out.

'What do you want?' she asked. 'Who are you?'

'I saw your mother in court this morning,' he said. 'Is she at home? Which flat is it?'

'Bottom,' said Elizabeth Crilling. 'Go on in.'

She walked past him into the road.

Archery went into the hall. Three doors led off it but they were all shut.

'Mrs Crilling?' he called. The place was hot and silent. He knocked on the middle door and opened it.

The room was thick with cigarette smoke, and everything in it was covered with dust or old newspapers. Mrs Crilling wore a stained[49], pink dressing gown and she was sitting in a chair by the window, looking into a garden full of weeds.

'Did you forget that I was coming, Mrs Crilling?' said Archery.

She turned round ... and stared crazily at him, her eyes seeming to burn right through him. 'Who are you?' she said.

'We met in court this morning,' he said. 'You wrote to me.'

She gave a long, high laugh.

'Mrs Crilling, are you all right?' he said.

She put a hand up to her neck and the laugh died away. 'Tablets,' she said. 'Give me my tablets and then you can ... you can get out!'

He saw the bottle of tablets on a dust-covered table and gave it to her. She did not open the bottle, just held it next to her chest. 'Where's my baby?' she cried.

Did she mean Elizabeth? 'She's gone out,' he said. 'Mrs Crilling, can I get you a cup of tea?'

'Tea? That's what she said this morning, the police girl. Come and have a cup of tea, Mrs Crilling.' She fell back into the chair, fighting for breath. 'You ... my baby ... I thought you were my friend ... Aaagh!'

Archery was really frightened now. He ran from the room into a dirty kitchen and filled a cup with water. When he came back she was trying hard to breathe. Should he make her take the tablets? On the bottle were the words: *Mrs J. Crilling. Take two when needed.* He took two from the bottle and pushed them into her mouth. She coughed over the cup of water but took the tablets.

He helped her sit up in the chair. 'I can be your friend,' he told her.

'Not my friend!' she said. 'Police friend! ... I watched you come out with them.' She screamed long and loud and he put his hands over his ears. '... Don't let them take her to prison!' Then she screamed again and began waving her arms wildly.

Archery was very frightened. He moved backwards out of the room, hurried though the hall and half-ran outside.

————

Archery stood on Kingsbrook Bridge, breathing deeply. After a moment, he looked round and was surprised to see the detective inspector standing next to him.

'Good afternoon, sir,' said Burden. 'Are you feeling OK?'

'I've just come from Mrs Crilling's,' said Archery.

Burden nodded. 'I understand.' They began to walk up the High Street until they saw a café. They went in and ordered tea.

'Did she get a bit excited?' Burden went on, when they had sat down at a small table in the corner. 'Did she have trouble breathing? It's all in her mind, Mr Archery. Next time you see her she'll probably be quite calm and friendly.'

'Tell me about the Crillings,' said Archery.

'There's a lot to tell,' said Burden. 'Josephine Crilling's husband died and she moved into the town and got a job. The child, Elizabeth, was always difficult but her mother made her worse. Elizabeth went to several different schools, and then when she was about fourteen she was put into a children's home. The court said that she needed to be taken away from her mother, but she went back after a time, as they usually do.'

'Did all this happen because she found Mrs Primero's body?'

'Perhaps,' said Burden. 'But Josephine Crilling was always a bit crazy. She was in Stowerton mental hospital once or twice, and then about four years ago she got a boyfriend. But the boyfriend decided that he liked Elizabeth more than her mother, and Elizabeth went to live with him. That was enough to send Josephine Crilling back into the mental hospital. When she came out, Elizabeth went back home to live with her mother. It was the boyfriend who gave Elizabeth the Mini.'

'Josephine Crilling is afraid Elizabeth will have to go to

prison,' said Archery. He thought for a moment. 'Perhaps Josephine Crilling did it. Perhaps *she* wore the raincoat and hid it. She was there.'

'Why would she want to kill Rose Primero?' asked Burden.

'People do strange things when they are mentally ill,' said Archery. 'At the trial she said that she went to the house the first time at 6.25pm. But was that the truth? Perhaps she went at 6.40pm after Painter had been and left, then she took the child back later.'

'To let her child find a body her mother knew was there?' asked Burden.

'Yes,' said Archery. '*Because nobody would believe that a mother could do something like that.*'

'You should be a policeman, sir,' said Burden, smiling.

'Perhaps,' said Archery. 'Alice Flower's next on my visiting list.'

6

Alice Flower

Alice Flower was eighty-seven years old. She lay in a narrow bed in a hospital room full of other old women. 'What did you want to know, sir?' she asked Archery. Her voice was soft but she spoke clearly. She was now almost as old as her employer, Rose Primero, had been when she was murdered.

'Can you tell me about the Primero family?' said Archery.

'Oh, yes,' she said. 'I went to work for Mrs Primero when the boy was born. Edward was her only child. It was very sad when he died, although he had a family of his own by that time.'

'Roger and his two sisters?' said Archery.

'That's right,' said Alice. 'Edward's wife – Mrs Edward, we called her – was left with very little money after Edward died. Mrs Primero wanted to help her, but Mrs Edward was too proud to take money from Mrs Primero.'

'Edward's son, Roger, was quite a bit older than his sisters, wasn't he?' said Archery.

'Yes, they were much younger,' said Alice. 'But there was only eighteen months between the girls' ages. Angela was the eldest. She must be twenty-six now. Then there was Isabel. They were only babies when their daddy died, but it was years before Mrs Primero and I saw them. Then one day Roger arrived at Victor's Piece. At that time he was working at a solicitor's office in Sewingbury. He didn't know that his grandmother was alive, but he'd seen her name and address in the telephone book.

'After that he came nearly every Sunday, and once or twice he brought his sisters with him. They were living in London. Roger was a really nice young man.' She stopped speaking,

37

and Archery watched her face become angry. 'Not like that murderer Painter!'

Archery moved nearer to her bed. 'That was a terrible day, Miss Flower,' he said, 'the day Mrs Primero died.'

'I'll never forget it,' said Alice Flower. 'I told Mrs Primero I would go and speak to him, but she wouldn't let me. "I'll speak to him in the morning," she said.'

'He did come the next morning,' said Archery.

'Yes,' she said. 'I was making Mrs Primero's lunch. I had just put the potatoes on the gas cooker, and I heard them arguing. They were in the living room. Suddenly, one of the potatoes fell onto the gas and there was a lot of smoke, so much smoke that it made me cough! Then I did something silly. I poured water on the flames and it made a loud sizzling[50] noise. Oh, the noise!'

There had been nothing about that in the trial transcript, Archery thought, excitedly – the sizzling noise, and the noise of Alice coughing! With that kind of noise she wouldn't have been able to hear a man go upstairs, search a bedroom and come down again.

'We had lunch and Mr Roger came,' Alice went on. 'It was about half-past five when Mr Roger said that he had to leave and he came down to the kitchen to say goodbye. Mrs Primero was having a little sleep in the living room. I called "Goodbye, Mr Roger dear. We'll see you next Sunday." Then I heard him shut the front door. Soon after, I went to church. Then Mrs Crilling came.'

'Tell me about Mrs Crilling,' said Archery.

Alice sighed. 'I never liked her. She was only interested in Mrs Primero's money. She thought that Mrs Primero would leave her some money after she died.'

'But Mrs Primero didn't make a will,' said Archery.

'Oh no, sir, and that worried Mrs Crilling! She told me we should get dear Mrs Primero to make a will. But Mrs Primero refused to do it. She wanted all of her money to go to Mr Roger and his two sisters, so there was no need to make a will, she said.'

'Mr Roger didn't try to get her to make a will?' asked Archery.

'No, he's a lovely person,' said Alice. 'After Mrs Primero died, he got his bit of money – three thousand pounds and a bit more. He told me he would look after me, and he did. He got me a nice little flat in Kingsmarkham and gave me two pounds a week. He was a businessman by then.'

'I thought that he was a solicitor,' said Archery.

'He always wanted to have a business,' said Alice. 'About two or three weeks before Mrs Primero died, he came to see her. He told her that a friend had offered to go into business with him. He would need ten thousand pounds, he said. Well, Mrs Primero told him she couldn't help him, because ten thousand pounds was all she had. "But you'll get your share after I die," she told him.'

'Roger didn't ask her to make a will then?' said Archery. 'He didn't try to get her to leave him all ten thousand, leaving nothing for his sisters?'

'No, sir! He was much too nice to do that!' said Alice. 'After Painter killed her, the money went to all three of them. Mr Roger is a successful businessman now and he often comes to see me.'

Archery thought Roger Primero sounded like a good man.

'If you see Mr Primero,' said Alice, 'will you give him my best wishes?'

'Of course I will,' replied Archery.

———

Archery got back to the Olive and Dove just after eight o'clock. He went down to the dining room soon after and he was surprised to see chairs all round the walls of the room, but there were no tables.

'There's a dance here later tonight, sir,' the waiter explained. He took Archery into the smaller dining room and Archery ordered his meal. He watched the dance band getting ready until the waiter brought his food.

Suddenly, something touched his leg. He looked down and saw a dog.

Then he looked up and the tall woman he'd seen earlier was standing next to him taking hold of the dog's collar. She and the man had just come in with two more people. 'I'm sorry,' she said to Archery.

'It's all right,' he said. 'I like dogs.'

'You were here at lunchtime,' she said. 'He probably recognized you. We call him Dog. He doesn't have a name, but he's very clever.' She picked up the animal and held him in her arms.

The waiter came across to them.

'Hello, Louis,' the woman's husband said to the waiter. 'My wife decided to come to your dance, but we must have some dinner first. Our friends have a train to catch, so if you could serve us quickly, we would be very grateful[51].'

The four of them all sat down and the waiter brought their food soon after. People were coming in to the dance now, passing Archery's table. The tall woman's husband got up. 'I'll take you to the railway station, George,' he said to his friend, then turned to his wife. 'You don't have to come, dear. Finish your coffee.'

When they had gone, the woman moved into her husband's chair to watch the dancers.

Seeing her alone made Archery miss his wife. 'Why didn't I ask Mary to come with me?' he thought.

The woman's voice made him jump. 'Are you staying long?'

'Just a few days,' he replied.

'We come here often,' she said. 'They have these dances once every month. I love dancing.'

'Would you like to dance?' Archery asked. Then he wished he hadn't asked – he was not a good dancer.

'I'd love to!' she said.

She was a very good dancer and, after a moment or two, he stopped worrying about his feet and just moved with her and the music.

'I don't know your name,' she said.

'Henry Archery,' he said.

'Hello, Henry Archery.' She looked at him. 'You really don't recognize me, do you?'

He shook his head, feeling embarrassed.

'Before I got married, they called me Britain's top model – Imogen Ide. I had the most photographed face in the country.'

What could he say? He didn't know her name or her face.

She laughed loudly, but it was a warm, kind laugh.

Archery smiled at her. Over her shoulder he saw Chief Inspector Wexford. He was with a woman. 'That must be his wife,' he thought.

'Here's my husband,' said Imogen Ide. 'This is Mr Archery, darling,' she said, introducing them.

'Can I get you a drink?' her husband asked Archery.

'No thank you,' he replied. 'I must go to bed.'

'Then I hope that we see you again,' said Imogen Ide.

The couple moved away and Archery went up to his bedroom.

7

'The Most Beautiful Dress ...'

The sound of the telephone woke Archery. It was his wife. 'I've had another letter from Charles,' she said. Archery looked at his watch and saw that it was nine o'clock. 'He's coming to Kingsmarkham tomorrow,' she went on.

'Is he coming here, to stay at the hotel?' asked Archery.

'Of course,' she said.

———

Burden was calling at 102 Glebe Road on police business, but the person he wanted to see wasn't at home. Number 24 was on the same side of the road, so he decided to go and have a talk with Elizabeth Crilling instead.

The front door of number 24a was closed, but not locked. Burden coughed and walked in. In the back room, Elizabeth Crilling was sitting at the table reading the local newspaper.

She looked up. 'Did I ask you to come in?' she said. Then she got up and walked into the kitchen.

He followed her and saw some empty pill bottles and another half-empty bottle on the kitchen table.

'Have you been ill?' he asked.

'They're hers,' Elizabeth Crilling said, picking up a packet of cigarettes.

'Where's your mother?'

'She's out.' She lit a cigarette, then said, 'Why was that vicar here?'

'He knows Painter's daughter,' answered Burden.

Her face went white. 'Painter who killed the old woman?' she said.

Burden nodded. 'Yes.'

She looked out of the window at the garden, but Burden could see her thoughts were somewhere else.

'I used to go and play with her,' she said. 'Mother never knew. She was always with the old woman. They used to talk and talk and talk. She used to send me out into the garden and one day I saw Tess ... Does she know about her father?'

Burden nodded again.

'Poor girl. Does she have a job?'

'She's a student,' said Burden.

'*Student?* I used to be a student.' She turned to him, angrily. 'What are you trying to do to me? Get out! Get out!'

———

After Burden left, Elizabeth Crilling began looking in a cupboard for something strong to drink. '*Why did he have to come here? Why did he have to remind me of it all again?*' she said to herself. She found a bottle of cherry brandy[52] in the cupboard and poured some into a dirty glass. Her hand was shaking and the red liquid went over the top of the glass and onto the bathrobe. '*Red everywhere. I remember it ... Oh, God! God! No! ... I had nothing pretty to wear, nothing to show to Tess. One day, Mummy was with Granny Rose and the man called Roger. Tess took me upstairs to see Auntie Irene and Uncle Herbert. Uncle Herbert was big. One day I heard him shouting at Auntie Irene. Then I saw him hit her. But he was kind to me. Mummy said that I had to have a party dress. It was strange, because there weren't any parties to go to, but Mummy said that I could wear it on Christmas Day. It was pink ... the most beautiful dress I had ever seen ...*'

———

Irene Kershaw's voice on the telephone sounded cold and distant. 'Your son has had an argument with Tess, Mr Archery,' she said. 'She's coming home tomorrow, so she must be upset.' When he said nothing she went on, 'Did you phone me for some special reason?'

'Could you give me your husband's business telephone number, please?' he said.

'Perhaps you two can meet and try and do something to help Tess and Charles,' she said. 'People are asking about the wedding and I can't answer them, it's very upsetting.' Archery said nothing. 'The number's Uplands 62234,' she said.

Minutes later, Archery was speaking to Kershaw.

'I want to write to Painter's army officer,' he said. 'He didn't come to the trial because Painter's defence lawyer didn't ask him.'

'I don't know the officer's name,' said Kershaw. 'But the War Office can probably tell you.'

The War Office was helpful. They told him that the officer's name was Colonel Cosmo Plashet. He was an old man now, living in Westmorland. Archery wrote a letter to him, then, after lunch, he went to the Post Office to post it.

As he was coming out, he saw Imogen Ide. She was coming from the shop next door with an armful of white flowers.

'Good afternoon, Mr Archery,' she said. She smiled. 'Would you be very kind and open the car door for me?' He hurried to help her. 'I'm taking these flowers to the church at Forby,' she said. 'Some of my husband's relatives are buried there. It's a very interesting old building.'

'Perhaps I'll go and see it later,' he said.

'Why don't you come with me now?' she suggested.

'I'd like that, thank you,' he said.

———

The short drive to Forby was beautiful – they passed through green and yellow fields and woodland. When they arrived at the churchyard[53], Archery followed Imogen around the gravestones, with the flowers in his arms. The churchyard was cool and pretty but quite overgrown[54] and not well-kept. Some of the older gravestones had fallen over and were covered in grass and plants.

44

'It's one of the oldest wooden churches in the country,' she told him. 'Why don't you go and look inside while I put these flowers on the grave.' She took the flowers from him. Archery went inside the quiet church for a few minutes, and signed the visitors' book.

When he came out into the churchyard again, he could not see Imogen Ide. As he waited, he walked between the gravestones and read the messages on them. One name caught his eye[P]. John Grace. He remembered Wexford speaking about a young man who had died in an accident before a vicar could see him.

JOHN GRACE
Died 16th February 1945
Aged twenty-one years
'Go Shepherd[55] to your rest;
Your tale is told.
The Lamb of God takes
Shepherds to his fold.'

Was it part of a poem? He didn't recognize it. He looked round and saw Imogen Ide approaching.

'It's an interesting place,' he said.

'I'm glad I could show it to you,' she replied.

'My son is coming tomorrow,' Archery said. 'So perhaps I'll bring him here to see the church. He's twenty-one, too ...' Then they both turned towards John Grace's gravestone.

'I'm ready to go now,' Imogen Ide said.

8

Ten Thousand Pounds

'I'm going to see Roger Primero at half-past eleven this morning,' Charles told his father. 'I phoned him before I got here last night. I'm sure there's something suspicious[56] about him.'

They were sitting in the hotel lounge. Archery looked at his watch. It was 10 o'clock already.

'You'll need to hurry. Where does he live?' he asked.

Charles sighed. 'Don't you know? He lives at Forby Hall. He thinks that I work for the *Sunday Planet* newspaper. I told him my name was Charles Bowman. I said that I was writing about top businessmen and wanted to do a story about him.'

Archery didn't approve[57] of tactics[58] like this but he said nothing. 'Well, Forby's only four miles from here. It won't take long to get there. Do you want to look around Kingsmarkham first?'

They walked up the High Street and over the Kingsbrook bridge.

'You're studying English at university,' Archery said. 'So tell me where this comes from: "Go, Shepherd, to your rest, your tale is told. The Lamb of God takes shepherds to his fold".'

'I've heard it or read it somewhere,' said Charles. 'Where did you see it?'

'On a gravestone in Forby churchyard.'

Charles sighed again. 'I thought you wanted to help me and Tess, and all you've been doing is looking round graveyards!'

Archery began to feel angry. Perhaps he should go back home and let Charles do everything, there was nothing special to keep him in Kingsmarkham. Then he stopped and put a hand on Charles's arm.

'What's the matter?' asked Charles.

'The woman outside that shop – she's Josephine Crilling,' said Archery, 'The woman that I told you about. I really don't want to talk to her.'

But it was too late, she was hurrying towards them.

'Mr Archery! My dear friend!' She smiled. 'What a lovely surprise!' She was quite a different Mrs Crilling from this morning.

'This is my son, Charles,' said Archery. 'Charles, this is Mrs Crilling.'

'How do you do?' said Charles, but gave his father a quick angry look before continuing. 'I've heard so much about you,' he said.

'Nice things, I hope,' she said. 'Now you *must* come into the Carousel café and have a cup of coffee with me.'

'We'd be delighted to do that,' said Charles. 'Until quarter-past eleven, anyway.'

They were the café's only customers, but for a short time nobody came to their table to take their order.

'You have a lovely son, Mr Archery,' said Mrs Crilling. 'And I have a lovely daughter. Aren't we lucky?' She had been speaking in a low voice. Suddenly she banged the table and screamed, 'Service!'

Charles jumped.

A woman came out of the kitchen. She was the owner of the café and she looked coldly at Mrs Crilling. 'I asked you not to come in here again, Mrs Crilling,' she said. She turned to Archery. 'What can I get you, sir?'

'Three coffees, please,' said Archery.

'What was I talking about?' asked Mrs Crilling, quite calm again.

'Your daughter,' said Archery, hopefully.

'Oh, yes, my baby,' she said. 'She was *such* a lovely little girl. I had a dear old friend who loved her, too, and *she* had lots

47

of money, *and* servants. She was very old, and many times she said that she wanted my daughter to have some of her money after she died. I thought nothing about it, of course.'

'Of course not,' said Charles. 'You weren't interested in her money ...'

She smiled. 'You dear, understanding, boy,' she said, then went on, 'But then the doctor told me that my husband had only six months to live. I said to my old friend, "You should make a will. A thousand or two thousand pounds would be a big help to my baby, and you know how happy she makes you." And what had her grandchildren ever done for her? I thought. Nothing!'

'But she didn't make a will,' said Archery.

'What do you know about it? Let me tell it!' she answered angrily. 'It was about a week before she died. I'd had the will form for weeks, and poor Mr Crilling was dying slowly. But would she fill it in? No, not her! Each time that I started to talk about it, that crazy old maid, Alice Flower, stopped me. But then she – the Flower woman – got a bad cold and had to stay in bed. I asked my old friend if she had thought anything more about the money. "Perhaps I should do something for Elizabeth ..." she said. Well, I ran to my house and got the will form before she could change her mind. I asked my neighbour, Mrs White, to be an independent witness to the will.

'Well, we got it written,' she went on. 'The grandchildren were going to get only five hundred pounds each. My little girl was going to get eight thousand pounds when she was twenty-one, and then there was a bit for the Flower woman. After that, I went to say goodbye to Mrs White as she left the house, then I went back for the will. I said that I'd keep it safe, and I did. And then – only a week later – she died!'

'Well, I expect that eight thousand pounds helped your daughter,' said Charles.

'No, it didn't!' Mrs Crilling shouted. 'The will wasn't legal. The stupid old woman had written extra things on the will when I was at the front door with Mrs White, so they hadn't been witnessed!' By now her voice had changed to a high scream of anger.

Suddenly the owner of the café came out of the kitchen and took hold of Josephine Crilling's arm. 'Out!' she said. 'I won't have you screaming and shouting in here!'

'She's crazy,' said Charles, after Mrs Crilling had been pushed out into the street.

'I did warn you,' said Archery. 'But we learnt a lot. Are you still going to see Roger Primero?'

'Yes, I am,' said Charles.

———

Archery had been waiting to see Wexford for half an hour. He turned to the police sergeant at the desk. 'Perhaps I could see Detective Inspector Burden?' he asked.

'I'll see if he's free,' the sergeant said, and went to find him. After some minutes, the sergeant returned with Burden.

'Good morning, sir,' said Burden. 'Mr Wexford is busy.'

'I've got something important to tell you,' said Archery.

'Yes?' said Burden.

Then Archery told Burden about the conversation with Josephine Crilling in the café.

'Most interesting,' said Burden. 'So, when Mrs Primero was murdered, Mrs Crilling thought that the will was OK?'

'Yes,' said Archery. 'She didn't say anything about the murder. But I thought this might be enough to get the case reviewed[59]?'

'No it's not, Mr Archery. We can't do anything, you do understand that?'

Archery tried not to be angry. What had he expected?

'Have you been seeing much of the country round here?' Burden asked, changing the subject.

'I went to Forby yesterday,' said Archery, after a moment. 'I was in the churchyard and I saw the grave of John Grace, the boy that Mr Wexford spoke about. Do you remember?'

Burden obviously didn't remember, but the desk sergeant looked up. 'I live in Forby, sir,' he said. 'We were quite proud of John Grace in Forby. He liked to think that he was a writer – a poet. He used to knock on people's doors and try to sell them his poems.'

'Was John Grace a shepherd?' asked Archery, remembering the writing on the young man's gravestone.

'No, I don't think so,' said the sergeant.

Burden went with Archery to the police station door. 'Did you speak to Alice Flower?' Burden asked.

'Yes, ' said Archery. 'Why?'

'She died yesterday,' said Burden. 'There's a report in the local newspaper.'

Archery found a newspaper shop. The *Kingsmarkham Chronicle* had the report on the back page.

Alice Flower was eighty-seven years old. She had lived in the area for twenty-five years, said the report. *For many years she was the maid and good friend of Mrs Rose Primero, who was murdered at Victor's Piece …*

A short report of the murder trial followed. Then: *The funeral*[60] *will be on Monday at Forby church. Mr Roger Primero has asked for a private funeral.*

'Roger Primero is still doing his best for Alice Flower,' thought Archery. 'I hope Charles has done nothing to upset that kind man.'

He went to the hotel dining room for lunch. He was finishing his dessert when his son walked in and dropped Archery's car keys on the table.

'I've had a most interesting morning,' Charles said. 'Anything happen here?'

'Not much,' said Archery. 'Alice Flower is dead.'

'Primero told me,' said Charles. 'Actually, it made it easier to get him to talk about the murder. Let's go out into the garden.'

As they found some chairs outside and sat down, Archery noticed that his son looked very happy.

─────

'First, Forby Hall,' said Charles. 'Mrs Primero lived there when she was a girl and Primero bought it this spring. A butler[61] let me in and kept me waiting for ten minutes before taking me into the library. Primero was there and he asked me to sit down and have a drink. Then his wife came in. We had our drinks and Primero began talking. I didn't have to ask much because he spoke about the murder quite naturally and said that he wished he hadn't left Victor's Piece so early that Sunday evening.

'Primero told me he had been going to meet a couple of friends that night at a pub in Sewingbury,' Charles went on. 'But he told me he hadn't seen them, because he went to the wrong pub. "I waited an hour, then went home," he said. What do you think about that? I thought it was suspicious. But what about the ten thousand pounds he needed to set up in business? Conveniently, Mrs Primero died and suddenly Roger Primero has his ten thousand pounds!'

'We know all this,' said Archery. 'Alice Flower told me.'

'Wait,' said Charles. 'Alice Flower didn't know this bit. Roger Primero said that he was very sad about what happened to his grandmother but that her death had been the start of his success. His wife was sitting listening, saying nothing, and he kept looking at her worriedly.

'I said, "So you got your ten thousand when you needed it?" Primero didn't answer, but his wife said "Yes. Ten thousand exactly. You should be asking me about it. Roger's told me about it so often that I know it better than he does."

'Well, I couldn't stop there. I asked about his two sisters, and whether they got ten thousand pounds, too. Primero began

51

'We had our drinks and Primero began talking.'

to look suspicious – I wasn't visiting to ask about this, after all – so I went on quickly and asked if they were successful in business, too. It was the right question because he relaxed after that. "I don't see them very often," he said. "Oh, Roger," said his wife, "we *never* see them." Primero looked coldly at her, then he said, "One is married, the other has a job in London, but they're much younger than me." After that he would only talk about his business. Then he asked me to have lunch with him, so I did. It was a very good lunch.'

'Alice Flower and Mrs Crilling both said that Rose Primero only had ten thousand pounds which she wanted to divide between her three grandchildren,' said Archery. 'But you're saying Roger Primero got all her money – the full ten thousand – and his sisters got nothing?'

'Yes. By law it should have been divided between the three grandchildren, because there was no will,' said Charles. 'So why wasn't it? Perhaps I'll understand when I see his sisters. The unmarried one, Angela, lives in London. Her name and address will be in the phone book, so it shouldn't be difficult to find because Primero's an unusual name. You could go to Victor's Piece and have a look round. Perhaps Roger hid upstairs instead of going out of the front door that Sunday night. Perhaps there's a hiding place.'

Suddenly, a shadow fell across Charles's face[P], and he put his head in his hands. 'Tess hasn't spoken to me for two days. I can't lose her, I *can't*. I don't care that her father was hanged for murder, but you do and she does and … oh, I can't expect you to understand.'

Then, without looking at his father, he turned and went into the hotel.

9

The Change in the Law

Angela Primero was twenty-six years old, and the older of Mrs Primero's two granddaughters. She lived in a flat at Oswestry Mansions in Baron's Court in London. That, and her telephone number, was all Charles Archery knew about her. He told Angela that he worked for the *Sunday Planet*.

As before, Charles said his name was Mr Bowman, and asked to meet with her. 'The death of Alice Flower has reminded people of Mrs Primero's murder,' Charles had explained to Angela Primero over the phone. 'Our readers will be wondering what happened to the other people involved in the case after the trial.'

Angela Primero had agreed to see him. 'But I don't remember very much about my grandmother,' she said.

When he arrived, he saw at once that she did not look at all like her brother. She had a plain face with bad skin, and flat brown hair.

'Come in, Mr Bowman,' she said.

Charles was pleased with the name that he had invented for himself and he smiled.

They went into a small room with very little furniture. There were no books, no flowers, just a few photographs of a young blonde girl and a baby.

She saw him looking at one of the pictures of the girl. 'That's my sister, Isabel,' she said. 'She's in my bedroom now, with her baby. She always comes to see me on Saturday mornings.' She nodded towards a chair. 'Please sit down. Now, what do you want me to tell you?'

'First, what do you remember about your grandmother?' he asked.

'Not much, as I told you,' she said. 'We went to tea a few times. There was a child across the road and we used to play with her sometimes. I never saw Painter but I think he had a daughter. I asked about her once, but my grandmother told us not to play with her.'

The door opened and the girl in the photograph came in. Angela Primero jumped up and took the baby from her. The child was about six months old.

'This is Mr Bowman, Isabel,' said Angela. 'Mr Bowman, this is my sister, Isabel Fairest.'

Isabel Fairest sat down. She was twenty-five years old, but seemed younger. She was small and thin with a pinkish-white face and large blue eyes. Her hair was the colour of gold. Roger's hair and eyes were black, Charles remembered, while Angela's hair and eyes were brown.

'About your early life, Miss Primero …?' Charles said.

'Oh, yes,' said Angela. 'I really can't remember any more about my grandmother. I was sixteen when my mother married again and she and my stepfather wanted us to go to Australia with them, but I didn't want to go. Isabel and I were still at school. After two years, they went to Australia without us and Isabel and I had the house. We both got jobs.'

She did not speak about money, or about her brother, Charles noticed.

'Isabel got married two years ago,' Angela continued, 'and her husband works for the Post Office. I'm a secretary in a newspaper office.'

'I like coming here,' Isabel said. She had a small, soft voice. 'It's so quiet. My husband and I have only got one room. It's nice and big, but it's noisy at weekends.'

'I'm surprised that your grandmother didn't leave you any money,' said Charles. He knew that he was taking a risk[P], but he had to get them talking about the money.

'That's life,' Angela said, in a hard voice.

55

Isabel touched her sister's arm. 'Shall I tell him?' she asked.
'Why?' said Angela. 'He won't be interested.'

'But I think that he should know the truth about Roger,'
said Isabel. She turned towards Charles. 'Grandmother left ten
thousand pounds. We should have had a share, but we didn't.
Roger – that's our brother – got it all. My mother had a solicitor
friend and he said that we could try and get our share by going
to the law, but Mother wouldn't do it. She didn't want to have
a court case against her own son. We were just little kids, and
knew nothing about it. Mother said that Roger would help us,
but he never did and we haven't seen him since I was ten and
Angela was eleven. I wouldn't recognize him now.'

'I'll tell you something, but I don't want to read it in
your newspaper,' Angela said after a moment. 'By law, Roger
was right to get it all, but it would have been different if my
grandmother had died a month later.'

'What do you mean?' asked Charles, trying not to sound
excited.

'Have you ever seen my brother?' she asked. 'He's little and
dark. Look at Isabel and me. We don't look like sisters because
we aren't sisters. And Roger isn't our brother. He's my parent's
child and Mrs Primero was his grandmother. But my mother
couldn't have any more children. They waited eleven years,
then adopted[62] me, and a year later they adopted Isabel.'

'But … you were legally adopted, weren't you?' Charles said.

'Yes, but adopted children can't inherit when the dead
person has died without a will. Well, they couldn't in
September 1950. The law was changed on 1st October 1950.
They can now. We were unlucky, weren't we?'

———

The photograph in the estate agent's window made Victor's
Piece look much more attractive than it really was. Archery
came out of the office with the house keys, and permission to
look around. He walked back to the bus stop by the Olive and

Dove, and waited. Minutes later, a silver-coloured car stopped by him.

'Mr Archery!' called Imogen Ide. 'I'm going to Stowerton. Can I take you anywhere?'

'I'm not going to Stowerton, just to a house near it,' Archery replied. 'A house called Victor's Piece.'

She looked at him strangely, and he guessed that she knew about the murder.

'You're not thinking of *buying* Victor's Piece, are you?' she asked.

'Why?' he said. 'Do you know it?'

'It used to belong to one of my husband's relatives,' she said.

Ide, he thought. What had happened to the house after Mrs Primero's death? Had someone called Ide owned it before it became an old people's home?

'I have a key and permission to look around,' he said. 'I'm not going to buy it. It's just – well …'

'You're curious[63],' she said. 'Perhaps you study old crimes? Actually, I think I'll come with you. I don't have to be in Stowerton until half-past twelve.'

She drove up to the front door. Even on this sunny morning, the house looked dark and mysterious.

Inside, the house was dark too, apart from the dusty sunlight that came through the hall windows. 'Be careful,' he said, and Imogen laughed nervously.

'That's the murder room,' she said, and pushed open a door. 'The stairs are behind here. On the other side is the kitchen where poor old Alice was cooking the Sunday dinner.'

Archery stood by the fireplace where Mrs Primero had felt the axe hit her for the first time and the blood had poured from her head. 'The scene of the crime,' he said.

The two of them said nothing for a few moments. Then Imogen Ide walked across to the window. 'You look very much like your son,' she said. 'Or he's like you.'

'I didn't know that you had met,' he said.

She didn't reply to this. Instead she said, 'You didn't tell me that he worked for a newspaper.'

Archery felt his face become hot. *Of course, she must have been there, at the Primeros' house,* he thought. Should he continue with Charles's lie?

'He looks just like you,' she continued. 'But I only realized it after he'd gone. I expect Bowman is the name he uses at the *Planet*. Of course, my husband hasn't realized.'

'I don't quite understand,' Archery began. 'Mrs Ide ...'

'Ide was my name before I was married,' she said.

He turned away. 'Was it your husband's relative who owned this house?' he said. 'The relative who is buried at Forby?'

She nodded.

'I've been stupid,' he said. 'Forgive me, I didn't realize ...'

She smiled. 'There is nothing to forgive. I should have told you that I'm Imogen Primero, Roger's wife.'

He walked away from her into the hall. 'You have to go to Stowerton,' he reminded her. 'It was kind of you to bring me.'

She nodded. 'Yes, I must go. It was nice to see you again. Goodbye!' She turned and walked down the hall and out of the front door.

———

The house was exactly the same as the description of it in the trial transcript. There was the long corridor that went from the front door to the back door where Painter's coat had hung. And there was the kitchen and the narrow stairs. Archery moved towards the back door, unlocked it and went outside.

The garden was very overgrown. The sun was shining and it was very hot, and the light and heat made Archery's head hurt. At first he could not see the garage, then he realized that it was in front of him, but its walls were hidden under a creeping plant. He walked across to it and pushed the door, but it was locked.

After some minutes, he walked to the road and a bus came almost immediately. He had forgotten that he had not locked the back door of Victor's Piece.

———

Archery returned the keys to the estate agent, then turned and walked slowly back to the hotel. The hotel lounge was busy with people having tea at small tables. Archery saw his son talking to a man and a woman – was it Mr and Mrs Primero? Their backs were turned towards him, but he saw that the woman had long fair hair and that the man's hair was dark.

As he moved towards them, the woman turned and he saw that it was Tess Kershaw. Tess was with her stepfather. 'Charles called in on^P us,' she said. 'When we heard his news, we came back with him.'

'News?' said Archery.

Charles told him about the conversation with Angela Primero and her sister. 'And then Tess, Mr Kershaw and I went to Victor's Piece,' he went on. 'Someone had left the back door unlocked, so we went in. We went all over the house and found several places where Primero could have hidden. He could have said goodbye to Alice, and opened and closed the front door without going outside. Then he could have gone into the dining room – nobody used that room, and it was dark. After Alice went out and after the coal was brought in, Roger could have come out, put on the coat that was hanging on the back door and – well, *murdered her.*'

'I don't know …'Archery began.

'Don't you *want* Tess's father to be proved innocent?' said Charles, angrily.

'I don't want Imogen's husband to be the killer,' thought Archery. 'He seems like such a nice man.'

'Tell me again about the money,' he said.

'Primero was working in a solicitor's office,' Charles explained. 'He knew the law and he knew that, with no will, all the money would come to him. But the old woman had to die before October 1950 because, after that, the law changed and his sisters would have got their shares of the ten thousand pounds.'

'What are you going to do?' asked Archery, after a moment.

'Wexford can't see me before two o'clock on Monday,' said Charles. 'He's away this weekend.' He stared at his father. 'Why are you looking so miserable?'

Archery could not tell him that he thought Roger Primero was a nice man. So instead, he said, 'I was thinking of those innocent children, the four little girls.' Then he smiled at Tess. 'I mean Tess, of course, Isabel and Angela Primero – and Elizabeth Crilling.'

10

Faces at a Funeral

Wexford looked across his desk at Roger Primero. 'What can I do for you?'

'You can catch a man pretending to be a newspaper reporter,' said Primero. He lit a cigarette, his hands shaking with anger. 'A man phoned me on Thursday and said that he worked for the *Planet* and he wanted to write about how I got started in business.'

'He came to your house and asked a lot of questions, but nothing appeared in the *Planet*,' said Wexford. 'So you phoned the newspaper and they'd never heard of him. Right?'

'How did you know?' said Primero. 'He seemed very nice. My wife liked him. I haven't told her about this because I didn't want to upset her. He was a tall, fair-haired young man and his name was Charles Bowman. He was very interested in my grandmother.'

Wexford almost laughed. 'Don't worry, I don't think anything more will happen,' he said.

'You think that he's just some crazy person?' Primero looked relieved.

'Almost certainly. Just forget about it.'

'All right' said Primero, after a moment. 'But I'll be more careful next time.' He stood up. 'I won't take up any more of your time[P]. I'm going to a funeral – poor old Alice.'

Wexford watched him leave, then he began to laugh – loudly.

***

There was nothing to do until two o'clock.

'Let's all get into my car and go to Forby,' suggested Kershaw. 'We could have a quick look at the church, then go on to

Pomfret. Pomfret House is open to visitors every weekday in the summer. Then we'll come back to Kingsmarkham.'

'Lovely,' said Tess.

Kershaw drove and Archery sat next to him. When they arrived in Forby, Kershaw parked the car by the village green, and the four of them sat on a seat on the grass. The village was quiet and pretty under the summer sun. Apart from the church, there were several cottages and just three shops – a post office, a butcher's and a place selling gifts for tourists. Kershaw took out his camera and began taking photographs.

Suddenly Archery knew that he did not want to go to Pomfret House to look at pictures and old furniture. 'I think that I'll stay here,' he said. 'I'd like to have another look at the church. I can go back on the bus.'

Charles did not look pleased.

Kershaw put away his camera. 'All right. Let's go.'

Archery watched them leave, then walked across to the tourist shop. 'Do you have a guide book for St Mary's church?' he asked the woman behind the counter.

'No,' she replied. 'But there are some in the church.'

There were some postcards on the counter and one was a picture of a shepherd with a lamb. He noticed it because of the words beneath the picture.

'*Go, Shepherd, to your rest ...*'

The woman saw him looking at it. 'That's by our local poet,' she said. 'He was just a young man when he was killed in a road accident.'

'You mean John Grace? I've seen his grave,' said Archery.

'Visitors to the village think that he was a shepherd,' she said. 'I have to explain to them that the word "shepherd" used to mean "poet". Do you want to see his photograph?'

She took some photographs from a drawer. They were all the same and under each picture were the words: *John Grace, Poet of Forby.*

Archery looked at the young man's face. It seemed familiar. 'Was any of his work published?' he asked.

'Only in magazines,' she replied. 'A publisher had a cottage in the village and he wanted to put the poems into a book, but then the boy died. Mrs Grace, the boy's mother, still wanted the publisher to do the book, but most of the poems had disappeared. She said that he'd written plays, too, but nobody could find them. Perhaps he burnt them or gave them away.'

Archery bought the postcard then he walked to the church and looked inside. A funeral service was just finishing so he closed the door and went to look again at John Grace's grave. Then he found a seat under a tree and sat down. It was almost twelve o'clock, twenty minutes before his bus to Kingsmarkham.

After several minutes, people began to come out of the church, with a man and woman at the front. They could not see Archery. They walked towards an open grave across the churchyard. The woman's back was towards Archery, but he recognized her immediately. It was Imogen Primero.

This was Alice Flower's funeral, Archery realized.

The people came together at the side of the grave and the vicar began to speak. Roger Primero moved forward and looked into the open grave at the coffin. His shoulders shook, and his wife put her hand on his arm.

Moments later, the vicar and Primero moved away from the grave and spoke together, then Primero took hold of his wife's arm and they walked towards the gate where several cars were waiting.

When they had all left the churchyard, Archery walked out to the road using a side gate. He was surprised to see Charles coming towards him.

'Pomfret House was closed,' Charles told his father. 'So we decided to come back for you. The car is on the other side of the church.'

63

The Primeros would be gone by now, thought Archery, but he was wrong. They were talking to a woman outside the churchyard gate and suddenly, Primero turned and saw Charles. Charles's face went white, then red.

'Well, well, it's Mr Bowman of the *Sunday Planet*,' Primero said.

Imogen Primero came over to them. She looked at Archery, smiled and said, 'Why, hello, I ...'

'Recognize him?' her husband said, nodding towards Charles. 'I shall need you for a witness, Imogen.'

'What?' said Charles, angrily.

'Roger, Roger ...' Imogen said, trying hard to keep smiling. 'You remember Mr Archery, we met him at the dance. This is his son. He's a newspaperman, but he uses the name Bowman for his writing. They're here on holiday.'

Charles looked at her. 'That isn't quite true, Mrs Primero. My father and I came here to get information.'

'I don't understand,' she said. She was looking at Archery. 'What information?'

'Perhaps you'd like to give your "information" to Chief Inspector Wexford,' Primero said to Charles. 'Shall we go and see him now?'

'I'm seeing him at two o'clock,' said Charles. 'I'll tell him two things, Mr Primero. One, that you cheated[64] your sisters out of their share of your grandmother's money. Two, that you hid yourself in Victor's Piece on an evening in December sixteen years ago.'

'You're crazy!' shouted Primero.

'Stop now, Charles!' said Archery.

'It isn't true!' said Imogen Primero. And then, in a small voice, she asked, 'Is it?'

'Of course it's true,' said Charles.

There was a moment's silence, then Primero shouted, 'It was all legal!' His face was hot and angry. 'Who *are* you?'

*There was a moment's silence, then Primero
shouted, 'It was all legal!'*

Without looking away from Archery, Imogen put her hand on her husband's arm. 'Let's go home, Roger,' she said. She was shaking. 'I hope that you enjoyed your time here, Reverend Archery, and that you got the information that you wanted.'

Then they were gone.

11

The Surprise Alibi [65]

'I didn't know that the Primero sisters were adopted,' said Wexford.

Archery, Charles, Tess and Kershaw were sitting in Wexford's office.

'Is that all that you can say?' said Charles.

'No,' said Wexford. 'I can say that I've seen Mr Primero. He also complained about your visit to his home. I said you could make contact with the people concerned in the Primero case – make contact, I said, not make trouble.'

'Oh, that,' said Charles. 'All right, I'm sorry. But I'm sure your people tell lies sometimes, to get information.'

'My people have the law on their side [P]!' said Wexford, sharply. 'They *are* the law.' He paused, then went on, 'Now tell me the rest of your story.'

Charles told him and Wexford listened patiently.

'Of course, you'll say that Roger had an alibi,' said Charles. 'You must have checked it and, after all these years, it will be difficult –'

'His alibi was not checked,' said Wexford.

Charles was surprised. 'I don't understand.'

Wexford stood up. 'Mr Archery, I'll discuss this and answer your questions.' He paused. 'But not with Miss Kershaw in the room.'

'I'll go and wait in the car,' said Tess. She turned to Charles. 'Don't you understand? He can't talk about my father with me here.' She touched Kershaw's shoulder and the two of them left the room.

Charles looked at Wexford. 'Why wasn't Primero's alibi checked?'

Wexford spoke slowly and clearly. 'Mrs Primero was killed between 6.25 and 7 o'clock on Sunday, September 24th, 1950. She was killed in Kingsmarkham. At half-past six Roger Primero was seen in Sewingbury, five miles away.'

'Really?' said Charles. '*Who* saw him? Some friend that he'd paid twenty pounds to say that he'd seen him?'

Wexford sighed. '*I* saw him,' he said.

There was silence.

'*You?*' Charles said at last. 'Why didn't you tell us earlier?'

'You didn't ask, and I didn't know that you suspected him,' Wexford replied. 'I was in a pub called the Black Swan to meet someone who had information for the police. I left the pub at half-past six and came face to face[P] with Roger Primero. I knew it was him because I'd seen him in court.

'Primero said good evening to me,' Wexford went on. 'He looked a bit lost, and later I discovered that he'd been going to meet some friends but had gone to the wrong pub. They were waiting for him at the Black Bull. Ten minutes after I arrived back here, I was called to Victor's Piece.'

Charles got up slowly. 'Thank you very much, Chief Inspector,' he said. 'There is nothing more to say.'

———

Tess and Charles began to argue as soon as they were all inside Kershaw's car.

'I don't mind, and my parents don't mind,' Charles said. 'Why can't we just get married and forget that you ever had a father?'

'Listen, I've been very lucky ...' Tess gave a quick smile to Kershaw. 'But it – it was wrong to imagine that you and I could be married.'

'You and I?' said Charles, coldly. 'What about the next person who wants to marry you? Will you go through the same thing[P] with him? I suppose you will only marry him if his father is a murderer too?'

'Oh, stop it, Charles!' said Kershaw.

Archery touched Charles's arm. 'I think I'll get out and walk to the hotel,' he said. 'I need some fresh air.'

'Me, too,' said Tess. 'My head hurts, I need some aspirin.'

Archery, Charles and Tess all got out of the car, leaving Kershaw to drive back to the hotel.

It was only a short walk to the chemist's shop and Archery opened the door. There were two people inside – the girl behind the counter, and Elizabeth Crilling. The two women were talking.

Archery waited anxiously by the door. Tess went to the counter. 'Excuse me, sorry,' she said as she reached across Elizabeth Crilling to pick up a bottle of aspirin.

'That's OK,' said Elizabeth.

Tess paid for the aspirin. Just then, a man in a white coat came from the back of the shop. 'Is there a Miss Crilling here, waiting for a prescription[66]?' he asked.

'Yes, me,' said Elizabeth.

Tess turned quickly and opened her mouth to speak.

'This prescription can only be used six times,' said the pharmacist. 'I can't let you have any more of these tablets until I get a new prescription. Perhaps your mother …'

'The stupid old woman!' said Elizabeth Crilling.

Tess closed her mouth, her face suddenly white. She pushed the aspirin bottle into her pocket and hurried out of the shop.

———

Elizabeth Crilling came out of the chemist's shop with the memories going round and round her mind[67].

'*The stupid old woman,*' she said to herself about her mother. '*I hate her! Everything bad that has happened to me started with her – beginning with the beautiful pink dress.*

'*I remember … Mummy was making the dress for me, working on it all day that cold wet Sunday. When it was finished, I was very excited. I put it on.*

'"We'll go and show it to Granny Rose," said Mummy, but Granny Rose was asleep and she didn't hear us knock on the window.

'"Try again in half an hour," said Daddy. He was lying in bed, white and thin. Mummy had stayed upstairs, reading to him.

'"You stay downstairs, Baby," she said to me. "But don't get your nice dress dirty."

'I didn't care that Granny Rose was asleep, but I wanted to show Tessie my new dress.

'I'll put on a coat and run across the road now, I thought. Mummy wouldn't come downstairs for half an hour. But I would have to hurry because Tessie went to bed at half-past six.

'Why did I go?'

As Elizabeth walked unsteadily home towards Glebe Road, her mind was full of questions and anger.

12

'I've Cut Myself!'

There was a letter waiting for Archery at the hotel. It was from Cosmo Plashet, Painter's army officer.

'I'll have to go and apologize to Primero,' said Charles.

'I'll do that,' said Archery. 'I'll phone them. I like them and I would like to make sure there is no problem between us.'

Archery went to his room and opened the letter.

Dear Reverend Archery,

My memory is not as good as it used to be, but I will try to help you. I was not asked to speak about Herbert Arthur Painter at his trial. I suspect that was because his lawyer realized that my words would not help him. Painter was not a good soldier, he was often drunk and fought with other men. Painter had been in the army for one year when he became part of my regiment[68]. Soon after this, we were sent to Burma, part of the Fourteenth Army. After about three months, a young Burmese woman was killed in the village near our camp. Painter was charged with her murder. He was found 'not guilty', so I should say no more about this.

In February 1945, six months before the war ended in the Far East, Painter became seriously ill. He was sent home to England and arrived in March 1945.

I have no further information about him, but I believe that he left the army soon after this because of his health.

Yours truly,

Cosmo Plashet

Archery read again the lines about the Burmese woman. *I should say no more about this ...* Did Plashet believe that Painter had been guilty of killing the girl?

Archery looked up, surprised that it was becoming dark. The clouds in the summer afternoon sky were black, threatening a storm. The rain started moments later, when he picked up the telephone and dialled a number.

'Forby Hall,' said a voice. 'The Primeros' home.'

Archery decided that the voice must be the butler's. 'I would like to speak to Mrs Primero,' he said. 'I'm Henry Archery.'

He waited a few moments. Then he heard Imogen Primero's voice.

'Hello?' she said.

'I want to apologize to you about what happened this morning with Charles,' Archery told her. 'There's so much to explain. Would it be easier to meet?'

'Well … all right. But you probably shouldn't come here,' she said. 'And I'm not sure that Roger will accept your apology.'

'I thought I would go back and visit Victor's Piece this evening. Would that be a good place to meet?' Archery suggested.

'Yes, it's close to our house. When I have heard what you have to say, perhaps I can make Roger understand.'

'OK. I'll have to get a key from the estate agent. It's locked,' he said.

'I've got a key,' she said. 'How about I meet you there at eight o'clock?'

Charles looked round the door as Archery was putting down the phone.

'I've apologized to the Primeros,' said Archery. 'I'm going to meet Mrs Primero later to explain.'

'OK,' said Charles. He was not interested now. 'Tess and her father are going back to Purley. They're about to leave.'

'I'll come down,' said Archery.

Tess and her father were standing in the hall, waiting.

'I wish that I hadn't seen Elizabeth Crilling,' said Tess. 'But I also wish that I'd talked to her.'

'Your lives are very different now,' said Archery.

'We must go,' said Kershaw. 'I know that you wanted to help, Mr Archery. But you couldn't.'

Charles was looking at Tess but she looked away from him.

'Can I write to you?' he asked.

'I'm going to Torquay, to stay with my aunt,' she said. She was trying not to cry.

'Give me her address,' said Charles.

'I haven't got a piece of paper,' she said.

Archery put a hand into his pocket and pulled out the postcard with the picture of the shepherd on it. She wrote the address on the back of the postcard and gave it to Charles without speaking.

'Come on, love,' Kershaw said to Tess. 'Let's go home.'

———

It was raining heavily and Archery had to run from the car. He pushed open the front door of Victor's Piece and went inside.

'Mrs Primero?' he called. 'Imogen!'

There was no answer. Her car had not been outside but he was sure that he was not alone in the house. He opened the living room door and looked in.

Who would buy this place? Who could live here, knowing what had happened ...? But someone must have bought it because there was a workman's coat hanging behind the back door ...

The old woman had sat here when she'd told Alice to go to church. Her eyes had closed and she had fallen asleep. Josephine Crilling had knocked on the window. Then *he* had come with his axe ...

'Sorry I'm late,' said Imogen.

Archery jumped and turned round.

'How did you get in?' she asked.

'The door wasn't locked,' he said.

'A workman?' she said.

'Probably.'

They went into the living room and he began to tell her about Charles and Tess. Her face grew hard when he came to the bit about the money. 'The money ...' he said. 'His sisters ... you didn't know about that?'

'I knew nothing,' she said. 'Except that he had two sisters who he never saw. We've been talking about it all day, but Roger can't understand that he was wrong not to help them. And he's afraid that Wexford will think it was a reason to kill his grandmother.'

'But Wexford saw Roger that night, in Sewingbury,' he told her. 'At six-thirty. Wexford knows it wasn't him.'

'Roger doesn't know that, or he's forgotten,' she said. She sighed. 'Are his sisters very poor?'

'One of them is,' he said. 'She lives in one room with her husband and baby.'

'Roger has agreed to let them have their share of the money,' she said. 'Three thousand, three hundred pounds each. Perhaps a bit more.'

She looked unhappy and Archery felt sorry for[69] her. He walked to the window and looked out. It had stopped raining.

'What will your son and this girl do now?' she asked.

'I don't know,' he said. 'I don't think that *they* know.'

'And what will you do?' she said.

'Go back to my life in Thringford,' he said.

She reached out her arm to shake his hand. 'Well, goodbye, Mr Archery,' she said. She went out, closing the door behind her, leaving him alone.

After some time, Archery went out into the hall. He turned and looked towards the back door – and saw that the raincoat was no longer there. Had it ever really been there? Yes, it must have been because there was rainwater on the floor by the door.

He walked down to it. The door was made of wood with small squares of glass. One of the squares was broken, and there was a hole in it which was big enough for an arm to go through to turn the key.

Archery opened the door and went outside. Everything was wet from the rain. He began to pick up the pieces of broken glass and put them by the wall.

Could he hear the sound of feet? Was Imogen Primero still here? He moved to stand up and accidentally put his hand down on a piece of broken glass. 'Oh! I've cut myself!' he said.

The scream was loud and long. Then a girl's voice cried, 'Uncle Herbert! Oh, God!'

There was blood on Archery's injured hand, but he still put out his arms to catch Elizabeth Crilling when she fainted[70].

———

'What are you doing here?' Archery asked her.

Elizabeth Crilling was sitting in a chair that he had brought from the kitchen. Her eyes were open now, but her face was still white.

'I had an argument with my mother,' she said. 'I've made myself a bed upstairs and I come here sometimes.' She looked at him. 'I saw the blood on you. Then you said the words that *Painter* said: "I've cut myself".'

'Was it your raincoat on the back door?' Archery asked.

'Of course it was,' she told him. 'I went out to get something from my car. When I came back, you were with that woman, Imogen Primero. I waited, then came back for my raincoat.' Elizabeth lit a cigarette and continued. 'Did you think that it was Painter's? That night Painter stood there, just like you. But he was holding a piece of wood. There was blood on it, and on him. "I've cut myself," he said to me. "Don't look, Elizabeth, I've cut myself".'

13

'She's Covered in Blood!'

Elizabeth's hand was shaking. She was speaking, but Archery could see from her eyes that, in her head, she was far away, back in the past.

'"Uncle Herbert!" I called to Painter. "I've got my best dress on. Can I go and show it to Tessie?" Then he turned round and there was red on his hands and his coat.

'"I've cut myself," he said. "Don't look, Elizabeth, I've cut myself."

'"I want Tessie!" I said.

'"Don't go up there," he said.

'"Don't touch me. I've got my new dress on. I'll tell Mummy," I said.

'He put his face next to my face. "Don't tell her, Elizabeth Crilling, or I'll find you," he said to me. "I'll find you and I'll do to you the same thing that I did to the old woman".'

'But you went back with your mother,' said Archery.

'I was five years old, just a kid,' replied Elizabeth. 'What did he mean? I didn't know – then. I was much more frightened of my mother finding out I'd gone to Victor's Piece. I didn't know that it was blood, I thought it was paint …

'Then we went back,' she went on. 'I wasn't afraid of the house. He had talked about the "old woman" and doing to me what he did to her. I thought that he meant Mrs Painter because I'd seen him hit her, and he knew that.

'I found the body. Did you know? God, it was terrible! I was ill for weeks afterwards. They arrested Painter, but I didn't know that – no-one tells children anything. I only knew that Granny Rose was dead and that he had made it happen. I was afraid to tell anyone because I thought he'd do the same to me.'

76

'Did you tell anyone later?' asked Archery.

'I wanted to tell my mother, but she wouldn't listen,' Elizabeth said. 'She told me to forget about it. But I couldn't.'

'Miss Crilling, let me take you home,' Archery said.

She was standing up now. 'You know Tessie, don't you? She's going to marry your son?'

'I don't know,' said Archery.

'She was the only real friend that I ever had,' Elizabeth said. 'I never saw her again.'

'You saw her this afternoon,' said Archery, quietly. 'In the chemist's shop.'

She stared at him. 'That girl with the aspirin?'

'Yes.'

'And the boy? Was he her boyfriend?' she asked. Archery nodded. 'I would never have told her who I was. I suppose it was because the chemist said my name.' She turned away. 'I'm going upstairs now. Give Tess my love.'

———

By the time that Archery found a doctor's house, his hand was hurting badly.

'First that dead boy at the car accident, now this,' said Dr Crocker, as he looked at the cut. 'It's not a very enjoyable holiday for you.'

'I want to ask you something,' said Archery. Without stopping to explain, he asked the question that had been worrying him all the way from Victor's Piece.

'The beginning of October?' answered Crocker. 'It would be very unusual.'

Archery nodded and got up. Then he thanked the doctor and went back to the hotel.

———

Charles was in the hotel lounge, writing a letter to Tess.

'What did you do to your hand?' he asked Archery. But Charles spoke again before his father could answer. He was

77

looking at the card with Tess's aunt's address on it, the one with the poem on it that Archery had bought in Forby. 'You asked me about this poem on Saturday. Well, I've remembered that the words are part of a play. There are songs in it, and this is the last verse of one of the songs.'

'Where did you see it?' asked Archery. 'In Oxford? In a library?'

But Charles wasn't listening to him. 'Where did you go tonight?' he asked.

'Just to have a last look at Victor's Piece,' replied his father. Charles nodded. He seemed to accept this quite naturally. 'Elizabeth Crilling was there,' Archery continued. 'She'd had an argument with her mother. She goes there sometimes. She's got a bed there.'

'Did you leave her there? A crazy kid?' said Charles. 'She could do something stupid. We should go and get her. We'll pick up her mother on the way and take her with us.'

Archery sighed and gave Charles his car keys. 'You can drive,' he said.

––––––

It was around 11 o'clock when they arrived at Mrs Crilling's house, but there were no lights on at number 24 Glebe Road. Charles rang the front door bell again and again.

'She's probably in bed,' said Archery.

'Can we get round the back?' asked Charles.

They went down the side of the building. Light came from the backs of other houses, but none from number 24. Through the first window, the kitchen and hall looked dark and empty. They had to walk through weeds and long grass to get to the French windows[71].

'They aren't locked,' said Charles, opening one of them.

'You can't just go in,' said Archery.

But Charles was already inside the room and, after a moment, Archery followed him.

'The light switch is by the door,' said Archery. 'I'll find it.' He felt his way along the side of the table, then went behind a large chair. 'Wait there!' he called. His foot had touched something. Clothes, *and something inside the clothes!* He reached down with his hands. *'Dear God ...'*

'What is it?' asked Charles.

Archery could not speak. His hands were wet. Charles found the light switch and suddenly light poured across the room.

Mrs Crilling lay on the floor between the chair and the wall. She had a stocking[72] around her neck, and she was wearing something long and pink. She had been strangled[73].

'But there's blood on her!' said Charles. 'She's covered in blood!'

Charles found the light switch and suddenly light poured across the room.

14

The Truth

'It's not blood,' said Wexford. 'It's cherry brandy. Couldn't you smell it?'

They had taken the body away and Archery was sitting in a chair in Mrs Crilling's living room. He was almost too tired to think.

'But why? Why did it happen?' asked Charles.

'Ask your father – he knows why,' said Wexford. 'I saw something like this sixteen years ago – a pink dress that a little girl could never wear again because it was stained with blood.' He turned to Archery. 'Where's the daughter? Where's Elizabeth?'

'Why do you think that I know?' said Archery.

'Mrs Crilling has been dead six or seven hours,' said Wexford. 'It's ten minutes to three now and you left the Olive and Dove at quarter to eight. Where did you go?'

Archery sat silently.

'Father ...' Charles said. When he got no reply, Charles turned to Wexford. 'She's at Victor's Piece.'

The next morning was grey and cool.

'Elizabeth Crilling came with us quite calmly,' Burden told Archery as they were walking to the police station from the hotel. He left Archery with Wexford in the Chief Inspector's office.

'Elizabeth strangled her mother,' said Wexford. 'Because you found the body, you'll have to come back for the court case.'

Archery sighed. 'Elizabeth Crilling found a body sixteen years ago,' he said. 'Why? Because of her mother's greed for the money from Mrs Primero's will, money that she would never have. Without that greed, Elizabeth Crilling would never have found the body all covered with blood. It was a memory that stayed with her for the rest of her life. Her mother never let her talk about those terrible memories, and Elizabeth grew to hate her for it – hated her enough to kill her.' Archery looked at Wexford. 'After I talked to her, I went to see Dr Crocker.' He gave Colonel Plashet's letter to Wexford. 'I want you to look at this.'

Wexford read it, then smiled. 'Now I understand.'

'I am right, aren't I?' said Archery. 'I've been to Forby, I've seen a photograph, I've got a letter and I've talked to a doctor.'

'Yes, you're right,' said Wexford.

'We were both right,' said Archery. 'Painter *was* a murderer, but Tess's father *wasn't* a killer.'

'Both are right,' agreed Wexford.

———

Irene Kershaw opened the door to them.

'I hope it's all right that we have come, Mrs Kershaw,' said Archery. 'Charles would like to see Tess.'

Irene Kershaw did not smile, but she let them come in. 'Tess has gone to the shops to get a few things for her holiday,' she said.

Archery had explained everything to Charles in the car. He told him he should find Tess and speak to her.

After Charles had gone, Mrs Kershaw took Archery into the living room. When they were sitting down, he said, 'I went to see a grave in Forby. You were born there, is that right?'

'A grave?' she asked. 'Oh, yes. Mrs Primero's grave is there.'

'Not her grave, John Grace's grave,' he said. 'Tell me, why did you keep all his poems and plays after he died?'

She did not answer, but he could see that she was suddenly afraid. Then she got up and went to a cupboard. She took out a large box and gave it to him.

'You can have them, but don't ask me about him!' she said. 'You want to know about Painter, my husband. I'll tell you everything that I can remember.'

'I don't want to know about Painter,' said Archery. 'I'm interested in Tess's father, and I know now that Painter *couldn't* be her father.'

She started to cry, and the sound went on and on.

'Mrs Kershaw ...' Archery said. 'Can I get you some water?'

At last she sat up and shook her head. 'Does Tessie have to know?' she asked.

He was afraid to say that Charles was telling Tess right now. 'It's not important now,' he said. 'People in England don't worry about things like that.'

'Tell me, what do you know?' she said.

'I know that you and John Grace lived near each other in Forby.' He continued, 'You loved each other, but he was killed. You were going to be married. You were going to have his child.'

She nodded, silent and embarrassed.

'You were afraid, so you married Painter,' said Archery. 'John Grace was killed in February 1945 and Painter got home from Burma at the end of March. You had known him before then. Perhaps his regiment was at Forby before they went to Burma?'

She nodded again.

Then Archery saw Mr Kershaw standing silently at the open French windows. How long had he been there? How much had he heard?

Archery went on. 'You got married, and you let Painter think that Tess was his daughter, but he suspected the truth. That's the reason that he never loved Tess like a father.' He paused, then said, 'Why didn't you tell Mr Kershaw?'

Irene did not hear her husband move into the room behind her. 'He never asked me about Painter,' she said. 'But he was so good to me. I had to tell him some of it. He said that he'd take me away and give me a new life. After that I *couldn't* tell him that Tess was – was illegitimate[74].'

Some movement behind her made her turn round. She saw Kershaw and cried out, 'Tom! Oh, Tom!'

———

Irene did not come downstairs again. Archery thought that he would not see her again until the wedding. Tess sat next to Charles, her hand in his hand. The box of John Grace's writing was between them.

'I feel so strange,' she said. 'I feel like a new person.' She pushed the box towards Archery. 'What can we do with these?'

'I could show them to a publisher,' said Archery. 'It's something that I can do to – to make things right[P] after all that I've done ...'

'Listen,' said Tom Kershaw. 'You only did something that I should have done years ago – talked to my wife. Painter wanted her to marry him before he went away to Burma but she said no. But I never asked her why she changed her mind when he came back to England. Also, she didn't want to tell Tess about Painter and the murder, but I told her. I even got angry with Irene when she told Tess that her father wasn't a murderer. But she was right, of course. John Grace *wasn't* a murderer.' He looked at Tess. 'But she'll talk to me now and she'll talk to you too, Tess. Let's go up and see her.'

'What can I say,' asked Tess. 'How can I begin? I don't want to hurt her.'

'Begin with your wedding,' said Kershaw.

'All right,' she said.

Archery watched them leave the room together.

'We must go soon,' he said to Charles. 'It's time we told all this to your mother.'

Points for Understanding

1

1 How was Mrs Primero killed? What was her family background? What family did she have when she died?
2 How did Mrs Primero recruit Painter? What were his work and living arrangements?
3 What was the disagreement between Painter and Mrs Primero about bringing up the coal to her house?
4 Who are Mrs Crilling and Elizabeth Crilling? How do they know Mrs Primero? What kind of relationship did they have, and what was their connection with her death?

2

1 Painter had an argument with Mrs Primero on the night she died. What does he say it was about, and how did it end?
2 What three reasons does Wexford give Henry Archery for not believing Painter's story?
3 What was the importance of Painter's raincoat? Where was it found?
4 What is Henry Archery's connection with Painter? What happened to Painter's wife after Painter was hanged?

3

1 Why is Mrs Kershaw worried about her daughter and Charles Archery getting married? What is Henry Archery's reaction to this?
2 Why does Mrs Kershaw say she does not want to talk about Tess's father? What does she say about life? What does she say about Tess's father?
3 What happens to Mrs Kershaw's necklace? Why? What does it tell us about her feelings?

4

1. This chapter is called 'The White Mini'.
   a) Who was driving the Mini?
   b) What has happened?
   c) Why is the driver of the Mini crying?
2. How does Henry Archery help the dying man?
3. How were Tess and Elizabeth treated by Mrs Primero when they were children? How have their lives changed since her murder?

5

1. How does Henry Archery help the Crillings in the courthouse?
2. Who is John Grace? Why is Wexford talking about him? What was John Grace talking about when he was dying?
3. What does Henry Archery's wife tell him on the phone?
4. Who does Henry Archery go and see that afternoon? What is the state of the house? What frightens him while he is there?
5. What does Burden tell Henry Archery about Josephine and Elizabeth Crilling's life and health since Mrs Primero's murder?

6

1. What new piece of information does Alice Flower give Henry Archery when he goes to visit her, about the day Mrs Primero was murdered?
2. What are Alice's feelings about Mrs Crilling? What does she say about Mrs Crilling, and Mrs Primero's will?
3. What does Alice think about Roger Primero? What does she say he has done for her since Mrs Primero's murder?
4. How much money does Alice say Roger Primero received when his grandmother died? What does she tell Archery happened between Roger Primero and Mrs Primero a few weeks before her death?
5. Who does Henry Archery meet at the Olive and Dove hotel that evening?

7

1 How does Elizabeth react when Burden tells her that Henry Archery knows Painter's daughter?
2 When Burden has left, what does Elizabeth do? What does she remember about Tess's father, Herbert? What does she remember about a pink dress?
3 Who is Colonel Cosmo Plashet?
4 Where does Henry Archery go with Imogen Ide that afternoon? What catches his eye when he is looking around the graveyard?

8

1 What has Charles done to arrange a meeting with Roger Primero?
2 What does Mrs Crilling say about the will?
3 What has happened to Alice Flower?
4 When he visits the Primeros, what does Charles find out about Mrs Primero's ten thousand pounds that is so important?

9

1 What physical differences does Charles notice between Angela, Isabel and Roger Primero?
2 Why did Angela and Isabel not receive any part of their grandmother's money when she died? What could Roger Primero have done to make sure they got their share?
3 Henry Archery goes to Victor's Piece with Imogen Ide. Who is she married to? How does he feel when he finds out who she is?

10

1 Why does Roger Primero go to see Wexford?
2 What does Henry Archery find out about John Grace when he goes to the tourist shop in Forby?
3 What does Charles accuse Roger of when they meet him at Alice Flower's funeral? What does he suggest about Mrs Primero's death?

11

1 Who is Roger Primero's 'surprise alibi'? Describe the circumstances.
2 Why do Charles and Tess argue in the car?
3 Can you describe Elizabeth's thoughts and feelings about the pink dress and her mother?

12

1 What does Henry Archery find out about Painter from Colonel Plashet's letter?
2 Why does Henry Archery call Roger and Imogen's home? What arrangement does he make with Imogen?
3 What do Imogen and Henry Archery discuss when they meet at the house? What seems to be her main concern? What does she tell Henry Archery that Roger has agreed to do?
4 How does Henry cut his hand? Why does this affect Elizabeth?

13

1 What did Painter say to Elizabeth when she saw him with blood on his hands? What did she think he meant? Why didn't she tell anyone?
2 Why do Charles and Henry Archery decide to go back to Victor's Piece to find Elizabeth? Where do they decide to go first?
3 Describe what they find when they arrive at the house at Glebe Road. What has happened?

14

1 What is Henry Archery's explanation of why Elizabeth killed her mother?
2 What does Henry Archery show Wexford? What do the two men agree that Henry is 'right' about?
3 What does Mrs Kershaw admit to Henry Archery about John Grace? What is her explanation? What does she give to Archery?

Glossary

1 **thriller** (page 4)
   a book, play or film that tells an exciting story, especially about
   something dangerous like a crime
2 **commit** – *to commit a crime* (page 4)
   to do something that is not allowed by the law
3 **pseudonym** (page 4)
   a name that someone uses that is not their real name, especially for
   writing a book
4 **honour** (page 5)
   the prize of a special title given by the Queen of England
5 **evidence** (page 6)
   facts, statements, or objects that help to prove whether someone
   has committed a crime. *Forensic evidence* is found by using scientific
   methods.
6 **clue** (page 6)
   an object or fact that someone discovers that helps them solve a
   crime or mystery
7 **capital punishment** (page 6)
   the punishment of being legally killed. *Hanging* is a way of killing
   someone by putting a rope around their neck and letting them
   hang from it, usually as a punishment. This type of punishment was
   suspended – officially stopped for a short time – in Britain in 1965
   and ended in 1969, at the time when this book was written.
8 **convicted** – *to convict someone* (page 6)
   to prove in a court of law that someone is guilty of a crime
9 **prove** – *to prove something* (page 6)
   to provide evidence that shows that something is true
10 **qualifications** (page 7)
   something such as a degree or a diploma that you get when you
   successfully finish a course of study
11 **corridor** (page 8)
   a long passage inside a building with doors on each side
12 **case** (page 8)
   a legal matter that is decided in a court
13 **in charge of** (page 8)
   if you are *in charge of* something or someone, you have control over
   and are responsible for them

14 *investigated*
  to investigate something (page 8)
  to try to find out the facts about something in order to learn the truth about it
15 *axe* (page 9)
  a tool used for cutting down trees and cutting up large pieces of wood, consisting of a long wooden handle and a heavy metal blade
16 *run-down* (page 9)
  in bad condition because no one has spent money on repairs
17 *inherit* – *to inherit something* (page 9)
  to receive property or money from someone who has died
18 *such* (page 9)
  used for emphasizing a quality in someone or something or for saying that something is unusual
19 *maid* (page 9)
  a woman whose job is to clean rooms, serve meals, wash clothes, etc in a house
20 *coal* (page 11)
  a hard black substance that is dug from the ground and burnt as fuel to provide heat
21 *supposed to* – *to be supposed to do something* (page 12)
  to be expected to behave in a particular way, especially according to a rule, an agreement or someone in authority
22 *will* (page 12)
  a legal document that explains what you want to happen to your money and possessions after you die
23 *trial* (page 13)
  the process of examining a case in a court of law and deciding whether someone is guilty or innocent
24 *solicitor* (page 13)
  in the UK, a lawyer who gives legal advice, writes legal contracts and represents people in the lower courts of law
25 *rough* (page 13)
  a *rough* place is not pleasant because there is a lot of crime or violence there
26 *vicar* (page 15)
  a priest in the Church of England
27 *fetch* – *to fetch something* (page 15)
  to go and get something

28 **threatened** – *to threaten to do something* (page 15)
to tell someone that you might or you will cause them harm,
especially in order to make them do something
29 **dismiss** – *to dismiss someone* (page 15)
to force someone to leave their job
30 **bonus** (page 15)
extra money that you are paid in addition to your usual salary
31 **jury** (page 16)
a group of people, usually 12, who judge a court case. Members of a
jury are ordinary members of the public.
32 **knocked her unconscious** – *to knock someone unconscious* (page 16)
to hit someone very hard, so that they fall or become *unconscious*
– in a condition similar to sleep in which you do not see, feel or
think, usually because you are injured
33 **panicked** – *to panic* (page 16)
to have a sudden strong feeling of fear or worry and be unable to
think clearly or calmly
34 **deliberately** (page 17)
with a definite intention, not by chance or by accident
35 **arrested** – *to arrest someone* (page 17)
if the police arrest someone, they take that person to a police
station because they believe he or she has committed a crime
36 **wondered** – *to wonder* (page 17)
to think about something because you want to know more facts or
details about it
37 **hedge** (page 17)
a line of bushes or small trees growing close together around a
garden or field
38 **manual** (page 18)
a *manual worker* or labourer is someone whose job involves physical
work using their hands
39 **stepfather** (page 19)
someone's stepfather is their mother's new husband in a second or
later marriage
40 **witness** (page 20)
someone who tells a court what they know about a crime
41 **well-kept** (page 21)
a *well-kept* place such as a house or garden looks good because
someone often works on its appearance

42 **pearl** (page 21)
a small round jewel that is white and shiny and that grows inside the shell of a sea creature called an oyster

43 **pedestrian crossing** (page 26)
an area where vehicles must stop for people who are walking across the street

44 **accuse** – *to accuse someone of something* (page 28)
to say that someone has done something wrong or committed a crime

45 **prayer** (page 28)
the words that someone says when they are speaking to God

46 **magistrate** (page 30)
a judge in a court for minor crimes

47 **bail** (page 30)
an agreement where you give money to a court so that someone is allowed to stay out of prison until their trial. If they do not return for the trial, the court keeps the money.

48 **well-dressed** (page 33)
a *well-dressed* person is wearing good and fashionable clothes

49 **stained** (page 34)
if something is *stained*, it is dirty with marks left on it

50 **sizzling** – *to sizzle* (page 38)
to make the sound of food cooking in hot oil

51 **grateful** (page 40)
feeling that you want to thank someone because they have given you something or done something for you

52 **brandy** (page 43)
a strong alcoholic drink made from wine. The *brandy* that Elizabeth drinks is made with *cherries* – small round red fruit – and looks like blood.

53 **churchyard** (page 44)
the area of land around a church where dead people are buried. The churchyard has a lot of *gravestones* – large stones that show the names of the people buried there and the dates they were born and died.

54 **overgrown** (page 44)
covered with plants that have been allowed to grow in an uncontrolled way

55 **shepherd** (page 45)
a man whose job is to look after sheep

56 *suspicious* (page 46)
   making you believe that something is wrong, dangerous or illegal.
   If someone believes that someone has done something bad, they
   suspect them.
57 *approve* – *to approve of something* (page 46)
   to have a positive feeling towards someone or something that you
   consider to be good or suitable
58 *tactic* (page 46)
   a particular method or plan for achieving something
59 *reviewed* – *to review something* (page 49)
   to study or examine a situation, policy or idea again in order to
   decide whether it is suitable or satisfactory
60 *funeral* (page 50)
   a ceremony that takes place after someone dies, usually including a
   religious ceremony, and the formal process of taking the body to the
   place where it is buried or cremated – burnt
61 *butler* (page 51)
   the most important male servant in a rich person's house, whose job
   is to organize the other servants, to welcome guests, to pour wine at
   meals, etc
62 *adopted* – *to adopt someone* (page 56)
   to take someone else's child into your family and legally make him
   or her your own child
63 *curious* (page 57)
   someone who is curious wants to find out about something
64 *cheated* – *to cheat someone out of something* (page 64)
   to get something that belongs to someone else by treating them
   dishonestly
65 *alibi* (page 67)
   someone who has an alibi can prove that they were somewhere else
   when a crime was committed and so can claim to be not guilty
66 *prescription* (page 69)
   a particular medicine that a doctor has told you to take, or a piece
   of paper that a doctor gives you that says what type of medicine you
   need
67 *mind* (page 69)
   the part of you that thinks, knows, remembers and feels things
68 *regiment* (page 71)
   a group of soldiers that can be divided into smaller groups called
   battalions and whose leader is called a colonel

69 **felt sorry for** – *to feel sorry for someone* (page 74)
   to feel sympathy for someone because they are in a difficult or
   unpleasant situation
70 **fainted** – *to faint* (page 75)
   to suddenly become unconscious for a short time, and usually fall to
   the ground
71 **French windows** (page 78)
   a pair of glass doors that lead to a garden
72 **stocking** (page 79)
   a piece of clothing worn on a woman's foot and leg
73 **strangled** – *to strangle someone* (page 79)
   to kill a person or an animal by squeezing their throat so that they
   cannot breathe
74 **illegitimate** (page 84)
   born to parents who are not married to each other

Useful Phrases

looks down on – to look down on someone (page 7)
to think that you are better or more important than someone else, or
think that something is not good enough for you

making my enquiries – to make enquiries (page 8)
to ask questions to get information about someone or something

it didn't matter – to not matter (page 18)
if something *doesn't matter*, it is not important

knew for certain – to know something for certain (page 19)
to have no doubts that something is true

caught his eye – to catch someone's eye (page 45)
if something catches your eye, you suddenly notice it

a shadow fell across [his] face (page 53)
used for saying that someone starts to be less hopeful or to be afraid

taking a risk – to take a risk (page 55)
to do something although you know that something unpleasant or
dangerous could happen

called in on us – to call in on someone (page 59)
to visit someone, usually for a short time

take up any more of your time – to take up someone's time (page 61)
to fill a particular amount of time when somebody is busy

have the law on their side – to have the law on your side (page 67)
if something is *on your side*, you have a particular advantage. If you
have the law on your side, what you are doing is legal and correct.

came face to face with – to come face to face with someone (page 68)
to meet someone, usually when you do not expect it

go through the same thing – to go through something (page 68)
to experience something difficult or unpleasant

make things right – to make something right (page 84)
to try to make a situation better after you have done something wrong

Glossary and Useful Phrases definitions from the Macmillan English Dictionary 2nd Edition
© *Macmillan Publishers Limited 2007* www.macmillandictionary.com

Exercises

Background Information

Read the notes on the author and the story then the following statements. Write T (True) or F (False).

1 Ruth Rendell was born in Sweden. _F_

2 She is interested in how people commit murders. ....

3 The Wexford novels are famous all over the world. ....

4 Her first book was published when she was 24. ....

5 The Wexford novels take place in a modern British town. ....

6 In 1965 murderers were killed for their crimes in Britain. ....

7 The murder happened in 1964. ....

8 One of the characters thought the man was innocent. ....

9 At the time, British society was divided into classes. ....

10 Rose Primero thought she was better than other people. ....

People in the Story

Match the names on the left with their descriptions on the right.

1 Herbert Painter		a	Roger Primero's wife
2 Rose Primero		b	Rose Primero's grandson
3 Roger Primero		c	a friend of Rose Primero
4 Tess		d	Archery's son
5 Irene Kershaw		e	Herbert Painter's wife
6 Elizabeth Crilling		f	a vicar
7 Josephine Crilling		g	the person who was murdered
8 Archery		h	the murderer
9 Charles		i	Irene's daughter
10 Imogen Ide		j	a childhood friend of Tess

Complete the gaps with the names from the list above.

1 _Charles_ wanted to marry Tess.

2 _____ was in love with John Grace.

3 _____ worked as a driver for Rose Primero.

4 _____ married when she was nearly 40.

5 _____ found Rose dead.

6 _____ wanted Painter to be innocent.

7 _____ used to be Britain's top model.

8 _____ had mental problems.

9 _____ got £10,000 when Rose died.

10 _____ thought that Painter was her father.

Vocabulary: Crime

Complete the gaps. Use each word in the box once. You may need to change the form of the word.

alibi	arrest	axe	capital punishment	case
clues	commit	evidence	investigate	prove
~~psychological~~	review	strangle	witness	

I am Chief Inspector Wexford and I am interested in the
(1) _psychological_ reasons why people (2) _____ crime.
One of the first murders I (3) _____ was the Rose Primero
(4) _____ . At the time, it seemed fairly simple. The man
who worked for the old lady killed her with an (5) _____ .
There was a lot of (6) _____ to show this and Herbert
Painter was (7) _____ and hanged. This was because
in 1950, Britain had (8) _____ for the crime of murder.
Elizabeth Crilling was only a child but she was a (9) _____
and saw Painter with blood on his hands. The other people connected
to Rose Primero all had (10) _____ which showed they
were not at the house at the time of the murder. However, some years
later, a man who was interested in the crime, thought there were

(11) _____ that showed that Painter was innocent.
He wanted me to (12) _____ the crime and try to
(13) _____ that Painter was not the murderer. Unfortunately,
before we could find out the truth, another murder happened and an old
woman was (14) _____ .

Vocabulary: Anagrams

Write the letters in the correct order to make words from the story.

1	LITIGATEMILE	illegitimate	a child whose parents are not married
2	EARTHTEN		to say you will hurt a person who does not do what you want
3	HERINIT		to receive money or things after someone dies
4	LIWL		a legal document that says what to do with your things after you die
5	LOCA		hard, black fuel you get from under the ground
6	AQUATICIFLION		exams or a course you pass, often needed for a job
7	INSPECTORRIP		a piece of paper from the doctor, which says what type of medicine you need
8	CAPIN		to suddenly feel worried so you are unable to be calm
9	BEADIERTELLY		intentionally, having planned it
10	SUBON		extra money you get if you have worked hard

Complete the gaps. Use each of the words from the table above once. You may need to change the form of the word.

1 Tess's father was not Painter. She was ___illegitimate___ .

2 Roger Primero _____ £10,000 from his grandmother.

3 Tess had a good education and got a lot of _____ .

4 After Painter had killed Rose Primero, he _____ and couldn't stay calm.

5 One of Painter's jobs was to bring in _____ to make the fire.

6 Painter said that Rose Primero gave him a _____ of £200.

7 He said that Rose Primero _____ to sack him.

8 Rose Primero did not want to make a _____ to say who would receive her money.

9 The doctor gave Josephine Crilling a _____ to get medicine from the pharmacy.

10 Painter cut his finger _____ .

Word Focus

Circle the word which is different. The words are all in the story.

1 Which adjective is NOT negative?
overgrown   rough   (well-kept)   run down

2 Which word is NOT connected to the law?
a magistrate   a tactic   a jury   a trial

3 Which word is NOT a job?
a witness   a butler   a solicitor   a maid

4 Which word is NOT connected to the church in the story?
a funeral   a prayer   a vicar   a friend

5 Which word is NOT connected to money?
to inherit   a hedge   a bonus   bail

6 Which word does NOT describe a feeling?
stained   suspicious   grateful   panicked

Useful Phrases

Match the verbs on the left to the words on the right to make phrases from the story.

1	make	a	a risk
2	look	b	in on someone
3	catch	c	the law on your side
4	take	d	enquiries
5	have	e	things right
6	come	f	through the same thing
7	call	g	for certain
8	go	h	face to face with someone
9	make	i	down on someone
10	know	j	someone's eye

Choose the correct phrase from the table above to match the definition.

1 for the police to ask questions _____ *make enquiries* _____

2 to know you are wrong and to want to make the situation better

_____

3 to do something that could be dangerous _____

4 to think you are better than someone else _____

5 to make sure someone sees you, or suddenly see someone, as they see you _____

6 to visit someone for a short time _____

7 to suddenly meet a person _____

8 to know that what you do is legal _____

9 to be 100% sure about something _____

10 to have the same experience as another person _____

Word Building: Nouns and verbs

Complete the table with the missing nouns or verbs.

NOUN	VERB
1 *threat*	threaten
2	adopt
3 qualifications	
4	prove
5	inherit
6 prayer	
7	accuse
8 prescription	
9	convict
10	investigate

Mark the stress on the words above.

Grammar: Modal verbs of deduction

Circle the correct verb form.

1 Roger Primero wanted Rose Primero's money, so he (could have)/ must have killed her.

2 Painter was found with blood on his hands, so he can't have / must have murdered her.

3 Elizabeth Crilling was only five at the time, so she can't have / might have done it.

4 Josephine Crilling thought she would receive money, so she must have / could have killed her.

5 Wexford saw Roger Primero in a pub at 6.30pm so Roger must have / can't have done it.

6 Roger, Angela and Isabel looked different, so they could have / can't have been related.

7 Tess did not look like Painter, so she <u>can't have</u> / <u>must have</u> been his child.

8 Alice Flower was cooking and coughing so she <u>might not have</u> / <u>must have</u> heard Painter going upstairs.

9 Cosmo Plashnet thought Painter <u>could have</u> / <u>can't have</u> killed a woman in Burma.

10 Rose Primero did not answer the door, so Josephine Crilling thought she <u>can't have</u> / <u>must have</u> been asleep.

Grammar: The past simple and past perfect

Complete the sentences using the verbs in brackets.

1 Before Painter ____*arrived*____ (arrive) Rose Primero ____*had fallen*____ (fall) asleep.

2 Before she _____ (die), Rose Primero _____ (not make) a will.

3 Painter _____ (be) in the army before he _____ (live) in Kingsmarkham.

4 Josephine Crilling _____ (try) to persuade Rose Primero to make a will before she _____ (die).

5 When Archery went back to Victor's Piece, he _____ (notice) that someone _____ (left) a coat there.

Grammar: Prepositions

Complete the sentences using the correct preposition.

1 Archery was interested ____*in*____ re-opening the murder case.

2 Painter's wife was afraid _____ him.

3 Charles was suspicious _____ Roger Primero.

4 Archery was curious _____ Victor's Piece.

5 The Primeros were grateful _____ being served quickly in the restaurant.

6   Archery was embarrassed .... Imogen Ide.

7   Archery was embarrassed .... not recognizing her.

8   Elizabeth was frightened .... her mother.

9   Archery felt sorry .... Elizabeth.

10 Archery apologized .... Charles's actions.

Making Questions

Write questions for the answers given.

1   Archery wrote the letter to Wexford.

   Who wrote the letter to Wexford? Who did Archery write the letter to?

2   Alice Flower was Rose Primero's maid.

   ....

3   Painter lived above the garage.

   ....

4   Elizabeth Crilling found Rose Primero's body.

   ....

5   Kershaw was Tess's stepfather.

   ....

6   Roger Primero worked at a solicitor's office.

   ....

7   John Grace wrote poetry.

   ....

8   Mrs Painter was frightened of her husband because he hit her.

   ....

9   Elizabeth killed her mother because she hated her.

   ....

10 John Grace was Tess's father.

   ....

103

Published by Macmillan Heinemann ELT
Between Towns Road, Oxford OX4 3PP
A division of Macmillan Publishers Limited
Companies and representatives throughout the world
Heinemann is the registered trademark of Pearson Education, used under licence.

A New Lease of Death

ISBN 978–0–230–42233–9
ISBN 978–0–230–42236–0 (with CD edition)

This version of A New Lease of Death by Ruth Rendell was retold by
John Escott for Macmillan Readers.
First published 2012
Text, design and illustration © Macmillan Publishers Limited 2012

Designed by Carolyn Gibson
Illustrated by Simon Williams
Cover photograph by Getty / Hans Neleman

Printed and bound in Thailand

without CD edition

2017	2016	2015	2014	2013	2012
10	9	8	7	6	5	4	3	2	1

with CD edition

2017	2016	2015	2014	2013	2012
10	9	8	7	6	5	4	3	2	1